CONTESTING: THE NAME IT AND CLAIM IT GAME

WINeuvers for WISHcraft

By HELEN HADSELL

The Woman Who Wins Every
Contest Prize She Desires

Completely Revised and Updated
1988

Top Of The Mountain Publishing
Largo, Florida

CONTESTING:
THE NAME IT AND CLAIM IT GAME

by HELEN HADSELL

Printed In the United States of America

Library of Congress Cataloging in Publication Data.
Hadsell, Helen
    CONTESTING:
    THE NAME IT AND CLAIM IT GAME
WINeuvers for WISHcraft The Woman Who Wins
Every Contest Prize She Desires. Rev. ed. of: The
name it and claim it game.
        1. Success. 2. Contests--Psychological aspects. 3. Rewards (Prizes, etc.) I. Hadsell, Helen. The name it and claim it game, with wineuvers for wishcraft. II. Title.
BF637.S8H2 1988 131 88-12345

ISBN 0-914295-66-7

For more information visit
http://www.TheWinningSage.com

TABLE OF CONTENTS

PART I

PART II

PART III

INTRODUCTION

An Exciting Challenge for You, The Reader: Learn How You Can Play the Game of Life Using Positive Thinking To Win.

You may find this a bold and egotistical book. I hope you do. You may also find ideas that can guide you in the transformation of your life. You can change from a loser to a winner; that is, if you want to change.

Why was this book written? It was written for men and women who are unhappy and dissatisfied with their present status. Most of all, it was written for those of you who are willing to challenge your present ideas about life, and change them when necessary.

Contesting: The Name It and Claim It Game

What is the key to success—the key that opens the Magic Box where all the goodies of life are stored? It resides in the mind: the vast computer that has the secrets of the universe, and life itself. So, much awaits us when we become aware of mind, and when we take control of it.

We can finally learn why things happen to us; what places us in control of our fortunes.

No person and no circumstance can disturb our inner peace. Fear and tension vanish when you use positive control. Heartache and headache are exposed and dissolved. Everything becomes right, when we learn to love in this new way.

You, possess all the capabilities for self-enrichment. You need only exercise these powers. As you begin, have no concern whether you are proceeding correctly. Just begin.

Helen Hadsell

Chapter
One

The
Name It
and Claim It
Game

Contesting: The Name It and Claim It Game

The Name It and Claim It Game

The truly successful person is the positive thinking one. The more you cultivate and control a positive attitude, the more successful you become. As you develop positive thinking, success replaces failure, until you no longer can fail.

No matter your past or present, you can change your future. Everyone has a different idea of what success is. To some, being successful in their love pursuits is the ultimate goal; some seek health and body-building programs; while others want fame and fortune; and then there are those who need huge homes, cars, and money as a determining factor.

Unfortunately, some don't know what they want. They scatter their desires into so many avenues that they never really accumulate enough energy to make anything manifest for them. They run hot and cold, up and down, in and out of projects, never really stopping long enough to analyze why they are not successful. They never fully accept the idea that, with a positive attitude and control, they can actually materialize anything they need or want on the physical plane.

The following personal experiences which I'll share with you, are not to tell you how great I am... but to clue you in on how great you are. There not a saying that tells you so: *"All these things that I do, you can do, and more."*

A number of years ago, my idea of success was to be able to enter contests and win, win, win. . . anything and everything that one could possess in this material world. I developed a desire, a goal, and a determination. I had read a book on positive thinking, and it left an indelible impression. So I was out to prove to myself that anything the mind can conceive and believe, it can achieve with positive thinking.

STEP NUMBER 1. Set a goal. If you *know what*

you *want,* you can *have* it. I must make one think clear in regard to entering contests, since there are sometimes misconceptions as to why and how one wins. I had no background, such as a writing talent, nor had I taken any writing courses at that time. I did not know any people who worked for judging firms. In other words, I had no "pull."

Contesting: The Name It and Claim It Game

My first experiment began when my husband expressed a desire to own an outboard motor, since he enjoyed fishing. He called my attention to a contest sponsored by a soft drink firm: the prizes were outboard motors. The requirement was to complete a sentence, in twenty-five words or less, stating why you like to take "Coke" on your outings.

My one entry was this:"*I take Cokes on outings because I'm a lone-wolf fisherman, and Coke is my silent partner. It contributes no yakaty-yak, only cool, refreshing enjoyment when called upon.*"

I came upon this idea when I imagined my husband, so I naturally wrote from his viewpoint. He certainly did like to go fishing by his lonesome; that is, until the two boys were old enough to enjoy fishing trips with him.

Three weeks after the contest closed, the phone rang, and a company representative informed us that we had indeed won an outboard motor!

I confess, that prior to the announcement stating that I had won, every time the thought crossed my mind about the contest or the motor, I "convinced" myself again and again that I would win. I was so determined to be positive, I even asked myself, "I wonder when they will let us know that we have won." I had no negative doubts, such as "I'll bet the contest is rigged." (I'd heard that one quite often.) Nor did I entertain the thought that I wasn't lucky, or that only clever people win. (Now how does one acquire cleverness? Why, one works at it.) So you see, I refused to entertain any negative doubts.

STEP NUMBER 2. Never entertain doubts. This nullifies all good, strong, powerful, positive currents.

The second contest I entered was a jingle-type, where one had to complete a last line. The prize was a second telephone installed in your home with the bills paid for a year. I thought about how convenient it would be if I could have a phone installed in the kitchen, since I spent most of my time in that part of the house.

When I sent off my three entries, I used the same positive thinking I had applied to my "motor win." I knew I would be a winner, and again I questioned how long it would take the company to inform me. It took five weeks after the contest closed before I received the letter telling me I was a winner. I had no way of knowing which entry actually won.

In the meantime, we decided to move into a larger home, and moved from Grand Prairie to Irving, Texas. The company that sponsored the telephone contest was kind enough to send a check, in lieu of the phone service for a year.

By now the family was quite impressed with mother, who had made two attempts at entering contests, and won both. In the next efforts to win contests, the family joined in.

Next, a request came from our daughter, then twelve years old: she wanted a bicycle. She called my attention to a contest advertisement in the Sunday paper's "Comic Section." The requirement was to name a pony. We got so carried away this time, that we submitted seven entries. She won a girls, blue bicycle, four weeks after the contest closed. We had no way of determining which one of the names actually impressed the judges, but we did have great fun in being creative and coining original, apt names. The following are the names that we sent: Foot-Prince, Him BUCK-too, Fancy Prance, Stirrup Dust, StanPedro, Twinkle Toes, and Prance Charmin'.

Our eight-year-old son, Chris, was next to put in his bid. He too, wanted a shiny, new bicycle. At that time, a candy contest was in progress, and the top prizes were bicycles. We were to complete, in fifteen words, why we liked their candy product. Again, we made a family project of writing ideas, and in this endeavor, we submitted four entries. Now the children were so sure we just had to win, that we all waited for the mailman to bring us the letter making it official. We now realized, it took from two to six weeks after the contest closed, before the winners would be notified. And, of course, he won the bicycle.

This time we were interested in which entry actually won. We came up with this method: we submitted the first entry in his full name, Chris Vince Hadsell; for the second entry, we used only, Chris Hadsell; the third signature was, Chris V. Hadsell; and the fourth was, C.V. Hadsell. This way we were able to determine the winning, fifteen words. They were: *"So colorful, so neat, so nice and plump, they're chewable pick-*

ups for midday slump. "(The letter telling him he won was addressed to the name we used to submit this entry.) We were describing why we liked candy-coated, licorice pieces. Children's contests are great to encourage family help.

This idea of *keying* entries was not original with us, as later we learned that quite a few contestants used this method to key their entries, and to learn which one of their "brain children" actually won the prize.

At this time, there were so many contests with so many prizes, one had a choice of what one wanted; which to enter. Perhaps, instead, we had only become more aware of opportunities for obtaining the things we would like to have in life.

I inject this for anyone who sees this as luck. The fact that we did win the first time we entered helped us gain confidence. There is a cliche' that goes like this: "If at first you don't succeed try, try again." Had I not won my first try, I feel certain my positive attitude would have urged me to continue to enter anyway.

I have since realized that with a positive-thinking outlook there is no failure, *only a delay in results.* (Thinkabout it.) The imaging faculty played a leading part in the goals I wished to achieve. So, I recommend, to play any game successfully, train your faculty of imagination.

18

Chapter One

If the prize appealed to us, we worked on that contest—to win. Suffice it to say, we won: bats, balls, radios, dolls, games, electrical appliances, and cash prizes. In other words, you name it and we claimed it. I was reluctant at that time, to vie for any contests that offered trips, because I was afraid to fly. I had already told myself that if I did win a trip, I would not take it. So I never gave that type of contest any consideration or energy. In other words, I was content with comforts like blankets, bicycles, and basics. But that soon changed.

The day our two sons, Dike and Chris, saw a contest for a trip to a dude ranch in Arizona, they said, "WOW, that might be family fun." I wanted to go, but flying was out of the question, however, we did enter the contest. To make a long story short, we won the trip. Again, this contest called for children to name a pony. We submitted the same names we used in the other pony-naming contest, and noted that this time, the name StanPedro was the winner. When the forms came about flight schedules, I requested we be allowed to go by train. I refused to go by plane. I did not realize it was a prepackaged deal for the winners, and fly, you must. When I refused, we were disqualified. We did, however, receive a nice, second-place prize of a movie camera. My sons were very disappointed, however.

When I had time to consider the immaturity of my groundless fear of air travel, I had to do some powerful, positive thinking to convince myself that planes are quite safe. I told myself I would enjoy flying, and in the future I would enter contests and vie for trips, because they would be fun. In other words, I was *connin'* myself for the big lift.

I finally convinced myself, with all that positive thinking, that the only way to go is to fly. I called this *The Die As You Fly* program, knowing my fears would die when I actually experienced the venture. In the meantime, I was scared stiff. What a challenge. What conflict. Wow!

STEP NUMBER 3. You can con yourself into anything, by repeating it over and over again, until you incorporate it into your thinking. That is the way it is. Sometimes it takes longer, but I have found it is a very effective, surefire method, once you incorporate it into your conscious-thinking program.

A family, dude ranch trip was offered again the following Summer in a children's contest, and this time, I informed the family, itwould be our Summer vacation. This particular contest was sponsored by a ranch style bean company, and it merely required one to submit one's name on the back of a label. It was a sweepstake-type contest. Of course, we won it, and of course, we flew. To say I did not have apprehension would be a big, fat lie. I recall that all during the trip, I was in an "in-fright" trance; convincing myself how great it was. (Who was I to tell the

family that if God had wanted us to fly, God would have given us wings.) The family had such a great time, that I could not deprive them of future, fun trips they were now anticipating. I also did further reprogramming and told myself that next trip, I'd open my eyes, and eat the meal served on the plane. (The children said the food was quite delicious. I faked sleep until we landed. Well, who's perfect?)

The next year, we won first prize for a family trip to Disneyland: my younger son, Chris, "the fly-hi-boy," insisted we win trips. (He is an Aries, and for some reason they are always in the air.) We bugged him to draw the ugliest bug he could conjure up for this big deal. Talk about excitement, that really was one of the many highlights in the Hadsell family's fun-'n-game times. The trip was so delightful, I could have kissed the judges and sponsors. (Imagine kissing *perfect strangers*. . .i still have never met one.)

May I say, in all our experience of contest winning, the prizes were always more than we had anticipated. If we won an appliance, it was always the latest model. The representatives from the companies were most kind, and usually we got things not included on the prize list. For example our trip to Disneyland stipulated a trip for a family of four—there are five Hadsells—yet they included all of us, gave us extra pass books for the park activities, plus a generous spending allowance. It was beautiful.

Contesting: The Name It and Claim It Game

Chapter
Two

Let Big Brother
Win This One...
He is More
Patriotic Than I

Contesting: The Name It and Claim It Game

Let Big Brother Win This One...
He Is More Patriotic Than I

After the five-day, family holiday on the dude ranch, and the Disneyland trip, the boys' appetites were whetted for more travel and trip wins.

The next opportunity that presented itself for a trip, and proved interesting to boot, was geared for high school students. Requirements were to com- plete a two-hundred-and-fifty-word essay on, "My Responsibility to America." Two winners from each state would win a trip to the nation's capital for three days of touring and listening to government officials. The contest was sponsored by the Rexall Drug Stores: I had noticed the blanks in the store one day, and brought one home.

That evening at the dinner table, I was explaining the contest to the boys, and elaborating on what an advantage it would be to visit Washington, DC. I asked which one might like to make the trip. They both thought it over momentarily, then Chris said, "Let big brother win this one. He is more patriotic than

Chapter Two

"Okay, deadline is eight days from now, so you better do some serious thinking, and get it on paper," I suggested.

May I say, that after several years of contesting, I was still the one that stimulated the interest it took to get rolling on a new one. The family pool of offering encouragement, suggestions, and ideas, plus their positive thinking, made it a most gratifying, family, fun-and-game activity.

Dike's entry was so sincere and warm, that when I read it, I could find only one mistake, and that was in spelling. In my estimation, it was a sure winner. Now, all that was required was for the judges to make it official.

That evening we had out-of-town friends for dinner. (Usually I let my husband, Pat, read over the gems of wisdom [our entries], before I licked the stamp and envelope, and sent them on their merry way to impress the judges.) That evening, I was in a *show and glow* mood, for I was quite proud of Dike's originality, sincerity, aptness of thought, and clarity of presentation (rules the entry would be judged on). I just had to share it with our guests. I asked if they would care to have a sneak preview of a winning entry that would win our son a trip to Washington, DC. At first they thought I was kidding, but after reading it, I could see they were impressed.

Contesting: The Name It and Claim It Game

When one of the guests handed the copy back to me, he asked, "Say, this is terrific, but how can you be so sure that it will win the trip?"

Honestly, one can get a bit weary with all the "Doubting Thomases" floating around. I hope for your sake, there are not too many in your environment.

Had I been a *gamblin'* woman, I would have made a bet. Instead, I said, "Give Dike your address, and he can drop you a card while he is in Washington, DC."

I'll never do that again, because it appeared that I might know the judges, or have some pull, and it aroused suspicion. So that's a NO-NO: *Braggin' before Baggin'*. Remember that.

Dike was notified he won the trip, four weeks later. He brought home many interesting experiences that he shared with us. (This was his first trip without the family.) I sent a newspaper story of his trip to our guests—just thought they should know.

"Anything he can do, I can do better," was now younger son, Chris' attitude. He had an opportunity to prove his creativity very shortly. A popcorn company was sponsoring a contest, asking children under fourteen years of age to draw an original picture of a popcorn man. Top prize was a free trip to the World's Fair for that child and one adult. Besides the expense-paid plane fare and three days stay at a downtown hotel, the winner would also receive one hundred and fifty dollars spending money. My, what an exciting opportunity. I'd get to go to the Fair with him I Things were *poppin'*, and plenty of "corny" ideas exploding, (we kept discarding), but when the nitty-gritty time came to concentrate on one idea, we came up with a winner. It was one of the three, top winners in the nation. So, that year we saw the World's Fair.

"Can you top this?" was then Chris' challenge to his brother, upon his return from the World's Fair adventure.

"Give me time, little brother," was Dike's reply.

Then it appeared on the scene, a trip just geared for Dike. He was to graduate from high school in June, and a month before school closed, the contest appeared. Ninety youths would be given the opportunity to tour Europe for six weeks. They would hostel all over the continent to remote villages by: train, plane, boat, and cycle.

The Wrangler Jean Company was sponsoring this one. The requirement was to write a fifty-word statement as to why you felt you could be a "Goodwill Ambassador" to Europe. He wrote his entry, then immediately got ready to travel, by getting his passport and required shots. When I say we are positive, I also mean we are prepared.

A day before graduation, he received the wire: he was on the winning team. The experience of the tour is still considered one of the special events in his life. He still corresponds with several youths he met on the excursion.

Upon his return, as Dike was sharing his travelogue, and showing us slides of the places he had visited, Chris announced, "Say, that sounds exciting, it's my turn to go to Europe next Summer."

A Clearasil contest made it possible for his wish to be fulfilled. The next July, he was jetting to Europe on what he called "a trip where only the elite meet, greet, and eat." It was first class all the way: he claimed he had never seen such plush places, and had such exotic food.

This particular contest was a sweepstake. The number of entries in this type of contest is fantastic: some have drawn as high as 300,000 entries. Only thirty youths, fifteen girls and fifteen boys, were selected. He too, had his passport and required shots in readiness, prior to the official notice of the win. If you've got a positive attitude, flaunt it, but only in the family environment.

As I stated earlier, all five Hadsells were in the act of winning contests by using a positive attitude.

Daughter Pam had her place in the fun, also. Her interest slanted toward recipes and art entries. She won cash prizes by submitting recipes to numerous national, as well as local, contests. It was one of her entries that won, for the family, a complete home library, consisting of the fifteen-volume set of *Childcraft* and the twenty-volume *World Book Encyclopedia.*

In an art contest, it was her talent that snagged a stereo\record unit for us. She supplied us with radios through her endeavors in creativity. Pam, at one stage of the fun-and-game, contest pursuits, declared, after winning five pairs of roller skates, "I get the impression I'm spinning my wheels."

Chapter Two

After submitting an entry and winning an elabo-
rate, electric train set for the boys, we offered encouragement by telling her she was really on the
tight track."

Contesting: The Name It and Claim It Game

Chapter
Three

All Things Comes
To Him
Who Waits

Contesting: The Name It and Claim It Game

All Things Come
To Him Who Waits

One year, before the Christmas HoliDAZE, my husband asked what I wanted for Christmas. At that time I needed an electric trypan. I was already en-joying a steam iron, thanks to Proctor Silex; a new toaster from generous Sunbeam; a new coffee pot presented to me from Corning Ware; and an electric blanket, compliments of General Electric. Oh yes, I also had an electric: knife, can opener, mixer, and toothbrushes from other sponsors.

Contesting: The Name It and Claim It Game

I told the dear boy not to buy a frypan, as I was positive I'd be winning one shortly. In that month, I'd entered a number of contests with priority on that particular win.

When Christmas morning, gift-opening time arrived, the big, square box under the tree, contained an electric frypan. My husband had bought one for me.

Between January 1st and 20th, I received letters from three, different sponsors; all congratulating me on my winning their prize of an electric frypan! How wonderful. I was now able to give them as gifts.

One Spring, I had the inclination to remodel my kitchen. I was giving all the cabinets a fresh coat of pale yellow paint. One morning after the mail delivery, I was leafing through a magazine, enjoying my morning coffee, when I noticed that there it was on page thirty-two: the Westinghouse contest display. Amid all the appliances pictured, I could see the stately, coppertone stove; a perfect addition, and a "must" for my kitchen, redecorating project. Somehow, my eight-year-old, white stove had served its purpose, and now looked ancient. I knew I could contribute it to the church auction to help raise funds for their projects. So, I neatly and discreetly, mentally found the perfect place for it.

Fifteen hundred prizes were offered in the

Westinghouse contest. The first ten prizes were complete laundry units. The second ten prizes were refrigerator-freezer units. The ten third prizes were colored stoves; other prizes were portable TV's and small appliances.

I disregarded all the prizes, but the stove. The rules said to write a twenty-five-word statement on why you liked Westinghouse products. I was so enthused, I submitted five entries that evening. This time I had a long wait, because I entered immediately. (Usually a contest is advertised and promoted several months before the deadline. After the closing date, there is a period of two to six weeks before the winners are notified.) In the meantime, I sewed curtains for the kitchen windows, and installed the new flooring I had won in a local drawing. Every time I looked at my stove, I visualized a new, streamlined, coppertone stove in its place.

At this time, I was acquainted with a number of people whose hobby was contesting. We would share ideas, discuss contests, and where one might be able to find blanks. We even formed a club that met once a month, so we could encourage one another.

One day, about five months after the contest closed, a friend called to inform me she had just been notified that she was a winner of a portable TV. Later, I heard from a number of Westinghouse winners in the area. I hadn't heard a thing.

I assumed my timing was off, but regardless of Westinghouse, I definitely would have that stove in my kitchen. I was so positive; I could almost touch it by now. That is how vivid and real it had become to me. I kept thinking of the phrase, *"Thoughts are things."* I was convinced that if enough positive mental energy is sent out, things eventually manifest in the physical. Another phrase that is most comforting, and one which should be incorporated in your thinking, is, *"Anything The Mind Can Conceive... And Believe.. .It Can Achieve."* I was out to prove it to myself, again and again.

In the middle of that week, I received a legal-sized envelope, with a congratulatory letter, and a check for $1,000. I was a second-prize winner in a spray paint contest, that offered all prizes in money. Talk about being elated! Don't you see? Here was my "stove," with money to spare.

When I get excited, the first thing I do is call my husband, so he can share in my enthusiasm. My opening statement is usually, "You'll never believe this...."

His answer is usually, 'Try me, kid, I haven't heard it all, yet."

I bought the coppertone stove, and had it installed the following day. I was so pleased with "Project Stove," you would have thought it had dropped from outer Olympus.

Ten days later, I received another letter. This one was from WESTINGHOUSE. It stated that in the process of awarding prizes, someone had overlooked sending me a notification of my third-prize win, a stove! I was stunned. If one is ever able to become unglued, this could have been the perfect time. The district manager called me several days later to ask when he could have the stove delivered.

I explained the recent stove purchase. "No, I didn't get the Westinghouse brand. I ran into a clearance sale of stoves at Sears, and found one almost like the Westinghouse model, and I was able to save $85.00 below the usual cost."

The district manager was most kind and understanding. If I had purchased a Westinghouse stove, the full retail price would have been reimbursed. This is how I obtained a new washer-dryer unit, in lieu of a stove. Now that wasn't too dramatic, because I hadn't really given a washer/dryer unit any consideration.

One weekend, we went to the Texas State Fair in Dallas. I became intrigued with the color TV's and their sharp, colorful, clear, crisp pictures. That's when I got the notion what our next project would be to win a color TV. I gathered all the positive thinking I could conjure up, turned on the imaging faculty, and replaced our then twenty-one-inch, black and white unit, with a color set. I discussed our next project with the family, and they all agreed that, "Color TV For 603" (that was our house number), was easy to mentally think about when TV entered our mind.

Then it happened, our first TV win. Chris won a

sixteen-inch, portable, black and white set, for naming a duck in a children's contest. About three weeks later, I won a fourteen-inch, portable TV in a local radio contest. That, too, was black and white. We now kidded one another and discussed that perhaps we were not concentrating on "color" enough. So we agreed to give *color* more thought.

The next opportunity that presented itself was a caption-contest. In ten words, we were to tell what a baby was saying. One of the newspapers was sponsoring this contest for humor. The only prizes offered were color TV's and portable black and white sets. This time, I was so positive I would win.

Of course I did, but alas, another black and white set. I refused to be discouraged at what one might consider a failure, and I would not give up. It got to be a big joke around the Hadsell house: "Mother is 'color blind,'" or, "She isn't 'color conscious.'" After two years of projecting for a color TV, I finally gave in and went out and bought a set. That really wasn't any fun. I know there are no failures, only a delay in results, but that delay was just flat out, taking too long.

The following January, my husband flew to California on business. He wanted me to accompany him so we could see some live TV shows. Sounded like great fun. We did have a fun time over the weekend, as we attended a number of live shows.

Contesting: The Name It and Claim It Game

On Monday, while he was transacting business, I had a free day. I chose to go to NBC Studios in hopes of having the opportunity to see or talk to Art Linkletter.

May I go off on a tangent and explain why I wanted to meet Mr. Linkletter, again? The year we won the trip to Disneyland, I extended my visit for a few days. A former neighbor had moved to sunny California and invited me to stay on, visit, and be her guest. Here was an opportunity to see some of the TV shows.

I had watched the "Art Linkletter Show" on occasion, and always found the program to be sincere, wholesome, and entertaining. I also had hopes of one day being on a program. (A female characteristic of mine. I'm a show-off.)

My friend was able to acquire tickets. The night before I was to visit the Studio, and watch the show in progress, I suddenly had a very, strong desire to be ON the show. While sleeping, I had a dream. It was quite vivid: It was Mr. Linkletter choosing me from a vast audience, and inviting me to be on his program. (Most interesting, because that is exactly how it happened.)

After the audience was seated, prior to the program, I was waiting for my dream to unfold, in reality. Mr. Linkletter came on stage; looked over the audience, and walked up to where I sat, amid hundreds of people present in the auditorium that day, he asked me, "Don't I know you?"

I guess I was speechless for a moment, because it was happening just like I had seen it in my dream. What an unreal feeling.

"No, this is my first trip to Hollywood," I replied. He asked if I would like to have a very special, Christmas present. But natch! I was then escorted into the spotlight, and a huge box was placed before me. I was to open it so home viewers and the audience could see my present. Well, it was quite a surprise. (No, it wasn't a color TV.) When I raised the lid, out jumped a little, ol' Santa Claus, which scared the YELL out of me. After regaining my composure, jack-out-of-the-box presented me with a beautiful watch. The program was aired Christmas day, so all my family and friends were able to witness my TV debut.

I was now a celebrity, so I didn't have to wish for that BIG DEAL any more. After the program, Mr. Linkletter came to where I was seated, and again, asked if I were sure we had never met before that day? Now you don't think I told him I dreamt about this. Of course, I didn't. Since that episode, I have done quite a bit of research and reading on telepathy, projection in dreams, and regression into past experiences of ancestors, etc.. I thought it would be interesting to get Mr. Linkletter's views on the subject. I, however, did not have the opportunity during my last visit. Perhaps, one day I might have the occasion. I hope so.

Now, let's pick up the story that I was sharing with you earlier: about visiting the NBC Studio. While taking the Studio tour, I noted a line forming at the side of the building. People were waiting to be admitted into the Studio to view a show being taped.

I asked how I could be admitted, and found myself in line with the waiting group. The name of the show was, "It's Your Bet." They were going to shoot five, half-hour programs that day. The following week, they would air them, one each day. One could be eligible for prizes if, number one, you were chosen by the camera that zoomed into the audience and stopped on you; number two, if the celebrity that was playing the game (it was sort of like ESP) could, in sequence, correctly answer three questions his mate had already submitted to the "MC," who was conducting the show. It's like the Show on TV today, called, 'The Newlywed Game." If all the answers were correctly given by the game participant, the audience player would receive the prize that was flashed on the board prior to the game. It could be a refrigerator, color TV, washer, etc., but it would be a major appliance. If they missed one, the prize would be of considerable lesser value: a portable appliance. If none were answered correctly, that would be your prize: nothing.

It sounded interesting, and certainly it was a challenge. Fun, fun. I had nothing to do until 5:00 PM, when I was to meet my husband.

While waiting, I became acquainted with a mother and her daughter, who were standing in line ahead of me. They began discussing the possibility of being chosen for one of the prizes. They were familiar with the program, I was not. They informed me that they had been entering contests for years, and had yet to win one prize. "Bite your tongue, Helen," an inner voice said. "Don't blow until you can show," it continued.

As I listened to their stories of failure, I realized why they hadn't won. It was obvious. Sure they wanted to win, but instead of being positive, they had doubt. Not negation or pessimism, but just enough doubt that they nullified any positive energy they might have had when they entered a contest.

I call your attention to this, because this is what most people are guilty of doing. They say they are positive, but somehow they don't retain this powerful energy constantly—until their wishes or desires manifest.

Contesting: The Name It and Claim It Game

Here was a perfect opportunity for a positive experiment. I wanted these lovely people to win their desires. The mother wanted a color TV, and the daughter expressed a desire for a new refrigerator. It was only then that I turned on full-blast, my concepts of how great I thought positive thinking was, and asked if they would like to play a game using positive thinking and visualization. They agreed, but I could sense they were thinking, "What have we here, a kook?"

In all fairness, I must admit the studio audience was not too large: as an estimate, I would say about forty-five to fifty people. So that was cutting the odds considerably. I told them to be passive, and not to project any positive energy until the item they wanted was flashed on the screen. When that happened, they were to know (think) they would be chosen by the house camera to vie for the prize, and be the winner. They agreed.

After being chosen, I suggested they look at the answers given by the partner playing the game, then mentally project that answer to the person that was to give the correct answer. In other words, simply play mental telepathy. I reassured them several times it was a game, and if the three of us followed the rules, they would win the prizes. "What have you got to lose? It will just make watching the game more interesting," I continued to explain.

Then the fun and games began. The first prize, which was projected on the board, was a silver service with an assortment of wine, and a year's supply of the wine. We knew that was not wanted, so we showed no concern. The next prize for the person in the audience to win was a color TV. I could see both of them perk up. The next minute, the house camera zoomed in on the mother. You better believe she was startled. She turned to give me a weak smile, as if saying, "Well, I'll be." The players on the stage did their part. I'm sure both mother and daughter sent the answers to the person playing, and of course, I did. All three questions were answered correctly.

The bewitched, bothered, and bewildered homemaker from Ohio, won her first prize: a color TV. The games went on, and prizes of no importance were offered. We were then informed there would be an hour break for lunch. The show would be continued after lunch. Three more programs would have to be taped. The three of us went across the street for a bite to eat. That is when the daughter asked the question I knew she was quite concerned about. Didn't I think the whole thing was just coincidence? I agreed that it certainly did seem that way. So, would she like to now win her refrigerator by coincidence?

Contesting: The Name It and Claim It Game

"Why yes let's do it again," she replied.

When we returned to the Studio, the crowd had tripled in size. When she observed this, one could sense she was concerned. Then she gave me a weak smile and relaxed. The first prize that flashed on the screen for the audience was her refrigerator. The person that the camera zoomed in on was none other than the surprised daughter. When the mental telepathy game began, it was amusing how swiftly the players picked up the answers. And, of course, she was the winner of the refrigerator. Well, what do you know, another coincidence. Perhaps. Only thing with me is, I flat never did believe in coincidences or accidents.

After that show was taped and completed, we had a ten-minute break before the next one would start. The mother and daughter then asked me what I would like to win. They assured me that they would help me. At that time, I was having so much fun helping with their projects, I already had my reward. They left.

I still had two hours to spend before meeting my husband, so I stayed to continue watching the game.

As I sat in the audience, I could sense the group. Not one, to my sensing, had a strong desire to win an appliance. Maybe they didn't need it, who knows. But I got restless and bored, until I remembered that my dear ol' mother had mentioned, several times in her letters, that someday, she would like to have a color TV. So, here I go again. The camera zoomed in on me. The correct answers were sent to the players. I will admit, I got a little concerned for a moment when one of the players was wanting to give the wrong answer. (Sigh.) He paused, and then came forth with the right one. Thanks to the lovely people on the panel, my mother is now enjoying a color TV.

Contesting: The Name It and Claim It Game

"Why, that's witchcraft," some of you might be surmising. Why of course it's not. Let's call it what it really is: *"WISHcraft.* "But let's analyze this situation: the prizes were there for anyone who wished for them; the players of the game had free will—they could accept or reject anything that was mentally suggested to them.

Question: What if several people were vying for the same prize—which one would win?

Answer: The one that emitted the most positive energy.

Question: Can anyone do this?

Answer: It is being done every day, in every way. It's about time you are made aware of it.

When I became aware of the powerful tool one has when using their mind with control, I incorporated into my consciousness, this phraseology,*"I will always use my power of the mind for constructive, creative purposes, for everything that is good, honest, constructive, and humanitarian. I will never use these powers of the mind for anything that is destructive or harmful to anyone. If that be my intention, I will not be able to function with these powers."*

This I am most sincere about, for in my continuing research, I am aware that this powerful energy can be channeled for physical healings, to encourage the depressed, and can be of benefit to anyone who asks for help.

Several years ago, I happened to read a mini-quote expressed by a man named, Frank Outlaw. I would like to share his words with you now.

"Watch your thoughts, they become words; watch your words, they become actions; watch your actions, they become habits; watch your habits, they become character; watch your character, for it becomes your destiny."

Contesting: The Name It and Claim It Game

Chapter
Four

Yes... Yes...

You Can

Contesting: The Name It and Claim It Game

Yes...Yes...
You Can

"I'm curious to find out if a pooped couple, with three kiddos, can recapture the rapture of Springtime ecstasy in their fat, forty, frustrated years?"

This is the entry I submitted in every contest that was offering a trip to Europe. I'd set my sights to fly high, and vie for a trip to Paris, France.

I began "Project Paris," the first of the year. I was anticipating celebrating my 40th birthday in Paris: I would be forty years old, the first of June, that year.

Back as far as I can remember, I'd heard how

picturesque, romantic, and exciting Paris was side-walk cafes, music, and relaxed, friendly, happy people. That's what prompted me to write the above entry. I wanted to go see for myself. Of course, my husband would accompany me. You know it takes two, a he and a she.

I was really curious to find out if one could recapture the rapture of Springtime ecstasy in the city of life, love, and the pursuit of something!

I realize now that anything one does is based on what he or she thinks; how much daydreaming or energy one projects toward their goal. In fairness, I must admit at the time of my "Project Paris," I was impressed and influenced by all the things I'd heard and read about it. So, I had already halfway convinced myself it could happen. Now all I needed was to get the body there to experience in the flesh, if you will, if the rapture could be recaptured.

I could go into a long declaration on what my idea of ecstasy means, but suffice it to say, it's a carefree, comfortable, cozy, cool, calm, and protected feeling. That, dear reader, is my idea of ecstasy.

A cola contest began shortly after the first of the year. It was just the contest I had been watching for. Top prizes were trips to anywhere in the world you wanted to go. The promotion layout had this question: "Where in the world do you want to go and why?"

I knew I wanted to go to Paris, I knew why I wanted to go, and I *knew* I was going to Paris.

I was not too concerned about which contest would make this possible. Perhaps it would come in the form of a sum of money, but this time I would wait until my target date of May 15, then purchase tickets.

When you win trip prizes, they usually are package deals, and must be accepted and taken by the *winner.*

I was not too concerned where in Europe any contest would take us, because once I was in Europe, there would be no problem flying to Paris. So, I decided I would enter every contest until I won, and I had six months to make this dream a reality.

I'd read someplace that the stronger your faith, the more power you have. Also, you should continue to use your "God-power" within you, since you then acquire more power. "You do not use up God-power," the statement said. "It is inexhaustible, like the air we breathe."

In recent years, I have been asked a number of times by students following the Eastern philosophy and vying toward "spiritual growth," if I didn't feel I was misusing "God-power" for material things? Also, they claimed if I continued to use this power, I would lose it.

My answer to this question must come from my

experience. I do not believe it is a misuse of mental power to desire material things. Nor do I feel that it is "God's Will" to punish anyone with pain, disease, and poverty. Perhaps I have a different God than people who have this belief. To my way of thinking, I like the phrase: *"Ask and you shall receive; knock and it shall be opened unto thee; seek and you will find."* I have yet to come across any restrictions that limit you by saying, "But don't ask for a trip, health, or a better job."

If your way of thinking puts the damper on this type of goal or desire, then, dear reader, that is only your concept. I could write several novels on the misconceptions people have due to environment, religious dogma, guilt feelings, and set ways in their thinking. It is not my intention to condemn their thinking, but I do say, if they have reached a point of "no return," and they ponder or look for reasons, they must sure\y come up with the tact that they must change their ways. To change your ways you must change your thinking.

There I go again, sandwiching in a sermonette in one of my fun-and-game projects. My son keeps a soap box available, for jest, for when I become "sermonettish."

Now let's get on with the "Project Paris." I want you to know the cola contest to which I submitted my entry did not award me a trip to Paris. They did, however, present me with a third prize, a Hammond Electric Organ. I did some serious thinking on that win. Here is the explanation as to why I feel I may have prompted the organ win.

Judges are nice people. Some are serious, some possess humor, and some have sympathy. I base this on the type of entries I've submitted and won in the past. One sometimes can write sad, glad, bad, and sometimes a little "mad."

Contesting: The Name It and Claim It Game

When the judges in the cola contest read my entry, I'm sure they found originality, aptness of thought, and clarity of presentation, or it would not have been considered one of the top major prizes. However, I feel when it came to the final judging, the group talked it over and was concerned I might be a bit "mad," or disappointed if they sent me to Paris and I didn't "recapture the rapture." Perhaps they surmised what I really needed was therapy, and what better way to get it than to play the organ? Could this be the reason why they awarded me the organ? I'll never know, but I can guess, can't I?

Now surely you don't think I was disappointed. Remember earlier I said there was never failure, only delay in results. This is how I felt about this contest.

As I stated, there are many contests going on all the time, but I was only interested in trips to Europe or cash award contests, so I continued to enter.

The next contest that interested me was sponsored by a men's sportswear company. They were only offering six prizes: six trips to major cities in Europe. The rules were to complete, in twenty-five words or less, what city you would like to go to.

I again submitted that I wanted to go to Paris and why. I also submitted another entry that I wanted to go to Venice, Italy. It was beyond Paris and prize-wise, it was the best deal one could win. The trip was first class, but for only one person

It was now May 1 st of that year, and we still had not heard of any trip I'd won. I'd won a number of minor prizes, but no trip. We did get our shots and passports, and we also questioned what was taking somebody, somewhere, so long to notify us.

Several days later was when our son, Chris, won a trip to New York for two. We were quite elated as we realized New York is halfway to Europe from Texas. We did not have much time left for my June 1st target date.

It was a week later when we got the telegram from the men's sportswear contest. My husband had iron the trip to Venice; he could leave immediately if te wished.

We did some fast "wheelin" 'n' dealin'," changing he first-class ticket to tourist class, and we were actually refunded money from the airline after book-rig passage for two. It worked beautifully.

Chris, my husband, and I flew to New York. We spent three days at the World's Fair, and went on to Europe, after we saw Chris on a plane back to Texas.

It was June 1st when my husband and I were seated at the sidewalk cafe in Paris, sipping wine.

Now I want all of you to know, YES, you can recapture the rapture" of Springtime ecstasy, although fat, forty, and frustrated.

Contesting: The Name It and Claim It Game

When our exciting trip (three weeks in length) *to* the enchanting cities in Europe came to a close, I again felt thirty, pretty, and flirty.

So it's a state of mind. I agree. But please don't knock it until you try it.

Chapter Four

Contesting: The Name It and Claim It Game

Chapter
Five

Now

Act Surprised,

They Expect It

Contesting: The Name It and Claim It Game

Now Act Surprised,
They Expect It

Little did I realize what was in the "making for taking" when I went to the contest club meeting after my return from Europe.

The group met the first Monday in September, shortly after I returned from my European tour.

I was now known as The Gad About," with the many trips I'd won in the contesting field. I might add, I also was "glad about" the many comforts and conveniences provided by the merchandise prizes I had won.

Contesting: The Name It and Claim It Game

"Can you top this?" seemed to be the question that now presented itself.

After I shared my trip experience with the members present, everyone expressed a desire that they, too, might win a trip to Europe.

When the announcement was made of current contests now in progress, I really perked up when I heard that the Formica Company was awarding a dream home in their building material promotion. Now to me, that could be 'The Livin' Beginning."

The Formica home that someone would win had been on display at the New York World's Fair. I must admit, although I attended the fair, I was not aware of the contest, nor their display. Perhaps I was too excited about our European tour.

The contest was promoting Formica products. All homebuilders in the USA, who built a home with a certain amount of Formica products, and who participated in the Parade of Homes, had the entry blanks and the rules.

In order to participate in the contest, the rules specified you had to be a family homeowner, and you must have visited one of the Formica homes participating in the contest. This was Monday evening, and the deadline was on Friday of that particular week-end. I was told that the only Formica home participating in our area, that had blanks for the contest, was in Garland, Texas, nineteen miles from Irving.

On the way home from the club meeting that evening, I kept thinking of the house—all new, modern, spacious. The more I thought about it, the better I liked the idea. It was made to order for me.

Tuesday morning when I woke up, all I thought about was the house. After my husband left for work, and the children were off the school, I tried to get on with my daily tasks. Call it hunch, intuition, or WISHcraft, I felt compelled to drive to Garland to register in the sweepstake.

It began to rain. I called a friend who also enjoys entering contests, and happens to live in Irving. I asked her' to drive to Garland with me to register.

"Sorry, I can't go Helen. I just washed my hair and it's a miserable day to be on the highway,"she said. I called another friend in hopes she might go with me. No, she was sewing, and didn't want to get out in the rain. She reminded me that the contest promotion had been on for almost two years, and it was a waste of gas and time at this late date. I then tried to bribe her into going with me, by telling her I would buy her a pizza for lunch. No success.

Next, I tried to talk myself out of going until later in the week, but I certainly did not dismiss the idea of entering. Somehow, the most important thing for me to do that day was to get in the car, drive to Garland, and register my name for that home.

I drove in the rain, located the Formica home, registered both my name and my husband's name. I then sat in the spacious living room as I admired the beautiful furnishings and mastercraft workmanship of the Formica features.

It was then I became aware that I would win the house. Don't ask me how. I just KNEW.

I took an entry blank home, and was re-reading the rules when I pushed the panic button. I'd signed my husband's name, and the rules stated the winner must have visited one of the Formica homes. He hadn't.

Do you know I insisted that he drive to Garland with me and familiarize himself with the house, so when the judges notified us, we would not be disqualified by not following the rules. I learned you can lose a major prize by goofin' and not following the rules.

I know a woman who entered a contest to win a five-room house of furniture. She really wanted and needed the prize, because they were then building a new home. She signed her eleven-year-old daughter's name to the entry she submitted. She was so interested in keying her entry to find out what she had written that might win, she didn't follow the rules that stated you must be an adult. When the judging firm called, and the daughter answered and told the judges she was eleven years old, that was

the end of that win. The mother later called the agency to explain she hadn't noticed the contest was for adults over twenty-one years of age. The judges were sorry she overlooked the rule, but they had to abide by the rules as the furniture company sponsoring the contest would not award their top prize to a child.

That same weekend, we drove to Garland, introduced ourselves to the builder, and reviewed the details of the house. When we returned home, my great expectations began to manifest. Active faith alone will impress the subconscious, and I wasn't going to miss a bet.

The following week, I decided the house would be furnished with hand-carved, Spanish furniture. Why not? I'd seen just what I wanted on one of our trips to Mexico. I asked my husband to draw up plans for the house. The boys also put in their wants and desires. They suggested we have a huge game room, one that would accommodate a full-size pool table, the organ we had won earlier, the TV center and music area, and several couches for informal entertaining. I expressed the desire that the kitchen and breakfast area be open to a patio garden. We got so specific, we were all projecting toward its reality.

Our next act of faith was to spend weekends looking at lots for the house to be built on. The rules stated we could choose a lot anywhere in the United States, and Formica would pay for the lot, too. We spotted three lots that would suit our purpose. We had a fun time on this project alone.

Six weeks passed and still no news. Then one evening, while I was attending a club meeting, the phone rang. My husband was there to answer it.

The judging firm that was handling the contest promotion was calling. No, not to say we had won any prize, just to ask questions. The formal procedure is to see if contestants followed all the rules.

Question: "Was H.B. Hadsell married, and a home owner?"

Question: "Did we visit a Formica home, and where?"

Of course, my husband could answer all the questions, because we had followed the rules.

This preliminary investigation does not mean that you have won the prize. We were informed this is necessary to avoid awarding top prizes to people who are not eligible because they hadn't followed all the rules. The Company also must be certain that there is such a person, and that he is not related to anyone working or conducting the contest.

We were excited after the investigation, and now questioned ourselves as to how long it would take them to make it official, that we were the winners

77

of their house.

A week later, on a Friday morning to be exact, I announced that we would hear of our house win today. I recall commenting on how I better get the house straightened up, in case the officials came early. Also, I'd have to make a trip to the bakery to get pastries to serve these lovely people. My husband decided to stay home from work that day, so he could be on hand for the big moment.

At 3 PM, the phone rang. The person on the other end of the line identified himself as one of the "big wheels" from Formica. Heavens no, he didn't refer to himself as a "big wheel," but logic will tell you they certainly would not send a "nobody" for a big deal like awarding a dream house. He was accompanied by a public relations man, whom I can only refer to as a ball-of-fire and a "most jet-up and go-blow and show individual." I really liked the fellow because it's the live wires that get a job done.

The "big wheel" asked if he and one of his associates (the ball of fire) might come to our home to discuss a contest prize for which we were being considered. "If your husband is not home this time of day, we will wait until later in the evening, as we wish to have both of you present," he explained.

I almost blew it. I was about to blurt out, "What took you so long?" Instead, I answered, "Oh, do come on out. My husband is home today and I have the coffee perkin'."

"NOW ACT SURPRISED, THEY EXPECT IT," was the instruction I gave my husband.

They came. We did.

When the glad tidings were verbally made official, the merry-go-round began. They informed us that there had been over two million entries for that sweepstake.

It took no time to get the home ready for the show. They approved the lot, selected the architect,

79

and incorporated our wishes in the house plans. The Formica team, the builder, and everyone connected with the Hadsell house were livin' dolls. They did so many, nice "added things" to please us. Now, every time I see any Formica products, I again, mentally thank this team of lovely people for turning our wishes into reality.

"What about taxes" is the first question people seem to ask.

Formica thought about that, too. They informed us that if there was any financial concern over taxes, they would help us with this so we would not be burdened by turmoil, or taxes, and turn against this good fortune. However, we were able to take care of the situation, and for the past years, have enjoyed our spacious, gracious, comfortable Formica fortress.

One of the nicest features about this beautiful home is the "carefreedomness" of work, worry, and waxing. Formica took care of us and now Formica takes care of itself.

Beautiful people, are you beginning to realize the power of positive thinking and active faith?

Change your expectations, and you change your conditions. Begin to act as if you expect success, happiness, and abundance. PREPARE FOR YOUR GOOD. Nothing is too good to be true;

nothing is too wonderful to happen; nothing is too good to last, when you have a positive attitude for your good.

Contesting: The Name It and Claim It Game

Chapter
Six

How To Be

Successful
Without
Really Trying

Contesting: The Name It and Claim It Game

How To Be Successful Without Really Trying

The following are a number of personal experiences to again relay what can happen when the ideas of security, health, happiness, and abundance are firmly established in the subconscious.

It means a life—free from all limitation ! It surely must be the "Kingdom," which Jesus spoke, of where all things are automatically added unto us. I say, "...automatically added unto us," because all life is vibration; the things which symbolize these states of consciousness will attach themselves to us.

In other words, 'Tune In." Feel rich and successful, and suddenly you will receive a gift or large sum of money.

My husband and I attended a company, Christmas party where a door prize of a tape recorder would be presented in a drawing. Everyone in attendance had heard of our phenomenal success in winning things. One man, prior to the drawing, jokingly announced, 'The Hadsells should be disqualified, because nobody can win when they enter a contest."

Of course, we won the tape recorder, and we didn't even try.

Why did we win? Perhaps our past accumulation of positive energy had something to do with the win. I recall the incident quite clearly: When we were aware what the door prize was, I simply expressed a desire that I might win it, for we had intentions of getting one as a gift for one of the children.

For this incident, I have no logical explanation, except to say, "'twas just plain ol' WISHcraft."

If you should happen to be resentful and envious (and admit it to yourself), say this powerful, positive statement: *"What God has done for others, God now does for me and more."* Repeat it until it becomes second nature in your consciousness, then all things you desire will come your way. Don't be discouraged if you have a desire, as I mentioned in the above personal experience, and it does not produce results as swiftly as the tape recorder win. Remember, there is never any failure, only a delay in results. There, I said it again.

Over the years, I have learned not to be disappointed in anything, anyone, or any goal I project. If it does not manifest as fast as I might wish it, say for example, I had not won the tape recorder, my attitude would have been: "Oh well, you win some, you lose some. I KNOW it was premature, but it is still coming to me."

Don't ever dismiss or nullify good, positive energy because you are disappointed. Acquire the attitude, "...guess I need a little more patience." It really does wonders for your peace of body, mind, and well-being. You WILL GET IT.

Somewhere I read this bit of advice that I find most apropos: "No *man gives to himself, but himself, and no man takes away from himself, but himself: The 'Game of Success' is a game of solitaire, as you change, all conditions will change.*"

MY SOW AND REAP PHILOSOPHY

Nine local area automobile dealerships and supermarket companies co-sponsored a contest.

One had to go to the auto showroom to view the latest model car which was filled to capacity with groceries. The person that guessed closest to the amount of the total sum of groceries, would win a $150.00 coupon book, which could be spent in the stores. Second-closest guess would win the use of a sports car for a week.

When I heard of this contest, I called a friend and asked her if she would like to accompany me to play the guessing game to win some groceries.

We began our "fun-and-game" day this way.

On our visit to the first dealer, we submitted our guesses and agreed that I had the correct sum, and I would win the $150.00 prize in that dealership. Our next stop, we jokingly designated that my friend would win the cash award from that dealer; the next place I would win; and the next one she would win.

I must again repeat, we were in a very happy mood, and had great fun playing the game of guessing. There were four places where I would win the first prize, and four places where she would win. When we came to the ninth dealer, she suggested, "Let's win for my neighbor who has five children, and could really use the $150.00 grocery money." We submitted our guesses in her neighbor's name, and concluded our fun-and-game day.

Winners would be announced on Saturday of that week. We decided to stay home that day to answer the phone, and we would call each other later that evening to check out our score.

One might say at this point, 'This is unreal," but let me assure you it is fact.

I had three phone calls that afternoon. Two informed me that I won their prize of a $150.00 coupon book. One told me, I missed the total figure by three cents, but I won the second prize—the use of their sports car for a week. My friend won the $150.00 prize at two dealers, and the neighbor,

89

whose name we submitted, also won the first prize of $150.00 from another dealer. The one dealer I hadn't heard from concerned me. I told my friend I had a hunch he was dishonest, because I was certain I HAD SUBMITTED THE RIGHT AMOUNT at that dealership. The more I thought of it, the more I felt compelled to follow my hunch.

On Monday, I called the place, and asked the secretary who answered the phone, "Who won the $150.00 grocery certificate book?" She told me the supervisor who was in charge of the promotion had taken care of that, and she felt the winner had already been notified.

I told her I would call back and speak to the supervisor, as I was most interested in who won the prize. Several hours later, I called again. This time 1 spoke to the man in charge. He informed me that the winner had been notified, but he forgot her name. It was somewhere on his desk, and he had a customer, so he had no time to look it up. I told him I would call back in an hour, as I was curious to find out who won. At this point, I felt certain that this man was dishonest, and I knew I would not drop the issue. When I called again, he curtly informed me a woman living in Irving, named Helen Hadsell, had won. The car dealership was in Ft. Worth. "How wonderful. I know her," I quickly commented before I hung up.

What choice did he now have but to follow through?

Two days later in the mail, I received the prize of the coupon book, with a note of this nature: "We are pleased to inform you that you are the winner in our contest." The postmark on the envelope indicated it was mailed after my telephone conversation.

The moral of this experience is: I did not entertain any negative ideas about anyone being dishonest, but when the strong hunch prompted me to investigate, I did, and I was correct.

In my experience of contesting, I have had only two instances when I felt the person in charge was not honest. Both were in local promotions.

It is amusing to think about dishonesty, for *"As you sow, so shall you reap."* The more I become aware of this well-organized universe we live in, the more I realize the perfection of this law. You really don't kid anyone but yourself, when you are dishonest. Although, at one time, you may feel you have pulled a fast one, sometime in the future someone will pull a fast one on you. This law was laid down for us centuries ago.

This raises the thought: Perhaps you are reaping what you once sowed; perhaps the reason the prize was withheld is for this law to be balanced for one of the past shenanigans you pulled. This is

Contesting: The Name It and Claim It Game

very possible, but again, I could only follow my intuition, and pursue the incident to my satisfaction, or dismiss it as not worth the effort.

Chapter Six

Contesting: The Name It and Claim It Game

Chapter
Seven

Hunches

Are The
Handiest
Things

Contesting: The Name It and Claim It Game

Hunches Are The Handiest Things

After we moved into our dream home, we had no more reason to "keep up with the Jones." We were the Jones.

My son, Chris (the joker), at the time sixteen years old, called my attention to the fact that he, at bog last, was in the surroundings he should have been accustomed to a long time ago. In other words, what took you so long? He now expressed a desire for a sports car, a "sharp,"new wardrobe, impressive rings and things to show how prosperous he was. He wanted to create a new image. Okay, I'll say it: he was a showoff. Or should I chalk it up as being a teenager, and if you have ever been around one, nuf said on that subject.

What a difficult time the little darlings can sometimes make for themselves. Seems like no amount of love, patience, attention, and understanding can reach them during one period of the "growin', blowin', showin'" syndrome.

Fortunately, this period is brief and one can always be comforted in the fact that this too, will pass. Again, let me reassure you, there are never any failures, only a delay in results. There now, does that give you hope? Anyway, this was the period Chris was going through. That might give you further verification that we are the typical family, nutty as well as fruitful.

But let's get back to Chris' desire, the complete list of items he was vying for. Would you now believe a contest appeared on the scene that answered all his wants?

The Union Carbide Company was sponsoring a contest for teenagers. Rules called for the design of a piece of jewelry that would appeal to the youth. Requirements were to use one or more "Linde Star sapphires" on the piece of jewelry you designed. The Company was plugging star sapphires.

I understood the contest was in progress for almost six months, and all art classes in the high schools throughout the USA were informed, and encouraged to submit their ideas. There were two first prizes, one for a girl and one for a boy. The big, first prize included a trip to New York for a week, to attend the national jewelry show. One parent could accompany their "genius-child," jewelry-designer winner." A star sapphire ring would be presented to the winner, a gold wrist watch, two pieces of luggage, a $1,000 cash award, plus a trip to the men's manufacturing firm to choose a Fall wardrobe of your choice. Now I ask you, how does that grab you for having "all your bags in one basket,"? I mean, "all your eggs in one basket." Don't you see, that contest was geared for Chris?

It was about the last week before the contest closed, when he got all fired up about entering.

What kind of entry wins, and what did he submit? The following are the incidents that led up to his win.

He discussed the ideas of the contest with the whole family, and came up with this: nearly everyone in high school, at that time, was either in a band, combo, or thought they could play a musical instrument of some sort. He first toyed with the idea of submitting a banjo, but after giving it more thought, discarded it. The reason being, if teenagers were entering the contest, somebody would surely send or think of a banjo. It was too obvious, and could be duplicated. He maintained the musical idea, and then the thought came: why not a staff with two notes and a treble clef. That would be a great idea for a tie bar, and would appeal to all the teenagers. Although the rules did not call for you to title the piece of jewelry you designed, he figured he would call it the "LINDE GO GO." It was a natural for his entry. He was so excited, he drew his idea on paper.

He was not artistically inclined, nor was he an art student, but that was not a specific requirement It included all high-school students. His enthusiasm was now on high. Then he yelled out, "I just had another great idea," as he headed for the garage and tool chest. He came back a few minutes later with a pair of pliers and a flexible piece of wire. He then commenced to shape the wire into a staff. He then made another trip for finer wire, to depict the lines where the notes would be placed. He puzzled for a minute over what might be suitable to represent the star sapphire that would be incorporated on the jewelry. He headed for the pantry, looked at the dried rice and bean assortment I had. He decided on two small dried peas. He then glued the whole thing together, sprayed it gold, except the peas, which he left a pale green. I don't mind boasting a bit here, because we were all quite proud of his workmanship and *"WINgenuity."*

Although the contest called for a drawn sketch, which he did, he also felt compelled to mail

101

in his "paste-up" idea. He mounted it in a jewelry box lined with black velvet, it looked quite impressive.

As far as I was concerned, he already had a prize for the amount of pleasure he derived from his creativity.

After he mailed in his entry, I got excited about getting to New York again. I bought a pale lemon-colored suit for our trip and shopped for new accessories, as I waited for the judges to notify him that he won the first prize.

On Monday, about two weeks after the contest closed, I woke up with the strong hunch that today would be the day we would hear from the jewelry design contest.

I was so positive, I would have made a small bet on it happening. The mailman came with no news in the mail, but that didn't discourage me. There could still be news forthcoming via telephone or wire.

We had planned on going shopping some-time that day to get Chris a pair of shoes. We had to do it before 5 PM, as he went to baseball practice at that time. Somehow, I kept postponing leaving the house, jas if I was stalling for time. Then the phone rang shortly after 4 PM. It was one of the judges from New York. Chris answered the phone. They informed him that they only had one question to ask, "Was Chris a girl or a boy?" His answer was, "I'm all boy." The next morning, we received the wire that Chris won first prize for his jewelry design entry.

My hunch paid off by staying home until the phone call, as we later learned.

While we were in New York, enjoying the prizes, praises, and fabulous places, the lovely public relation's people took us to meet one of the judges. (This was after the prize had been awarded.) They wanted to meet the two, top teenage designers.

One of the judges, a woman, explained how difficult it was in making the top award selections. She told us that there was no question about the girl winner, but the final judging of the top teen-boy entry proved a challenge. The final decision was between a boy named Mike who, incidentally, submitted a "banjo" as his entry, and Chris for a musical staff presentation. When the nitty-gritty time came to select one winner, the judges were tired after several days of studying all the entries, and it was still a tie between Chris and Mike. The woman judge wanted Chris to win, because she was so impressed that anyone would take the extra trouble to submit an actual paste-up. The men judges tried to get her to agree with them, and give Mike the prize. They were certain Mike was a boy. They were concerned that if they awarded it to Chris, and Chris was a girl, they would have two girl winners.

So they did have a consideration. The woman judge said she finally agreed to complete the judging, but on one condition. She insisted that they call this kid from Texas. "If he answers the phone and tells us he is a boy, he gets the prize. If no one answers, I will concede to let Mike be the winner." They agreed, as they wanted to conclude their judging that afternoon.

Well, Chris was home, he answered the phone, he is a boy, and he was the winner.

This incident again, should convince you that when you have a hunch, and it makes sense, follow it. In my personal experience, it pays off ten out of ten times.

What an opportunity that was for Chris. From desiring to acquiring his wishes, took only four weeks.

This prize win and experience were two more of the Hadsell's highlights.

Chapter Seven

Contesting: The Name It and Claim It Game

Chapter Eight

The Supreme Test

Contesting: The Name It and Claim It Game

The
Supreme
Test

Now just what makes you think I should limit my positive thinking to contest wins? I admit I had my beginning with the will-to-win-contests' goal, but then something exciting happened to open a whole, new concept for me.

It was shortly after we moved into the house. At the insistence of one of my friends, we drove to Fort Worth to hear a man from Laredo, Texas. His name was, JOSE' SILVA. Mr. Silva was lecturing on the power of the mind. He told how one could control habits, weight, sleep without drugs, and a lot of good things. He offered a 48-hour course which included techniques of mental imagery for better health, better memory, superior intuition, and productivity, also how one could control pain. The man was so sincere, and as I listened to him explain one's mind potential, I knew I had to take this course. Why, I got so excited I could hardly wait until the following evening to begin class training. That, dear reader, was the best investment I have ever made to date. Four months after completing the SILVA MIND DEVELOPMENT course, I had the occasion to give the techniques I had been taught by Jose' Silva the supreme test.

My husband and I were involved in an auto-mobile accident one evening, on a slick, sleet-covered bridge. My face was thrown against the dashboard, as a car hit us head-on. The impact flattened my nose, caused internal facial damage, and I was unable to breathe due to the great amount of blood I was swallowing. I had two choices, to push the panic button and bleed to death, or stop the bleeding.

Dear reader, let me now confess that in the past, I probably was one of the most difficult patients with whom the medical profession had coped. I went into hysterics at the sight of blood. Just going to the hospital to visit a friend made me sick to my stomach, perhaps I sensed the fear and pain. I also had so many fears of dying, sickness, and pain, I frankly could have been labeled a prize neurotic.

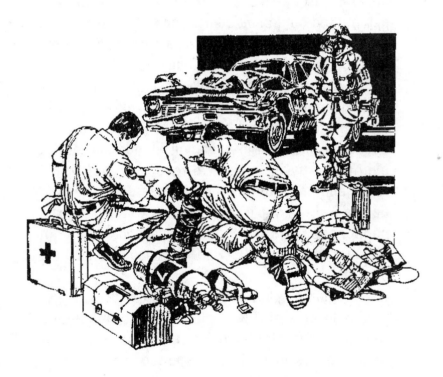

Seems like every time I heard some person relate their experiences of surgery or pain, I incorporated it into my consciousness, "HOOK, LINE, AND

THINKER."

Let's get on with the accident experience because WOW I was I fortunate. When it occurred, I was clued in on how to handle the situation, thanks to the SILVA MIND DEVELOPMENT program. One of the techniques we were taught in the Course was to stop and control bleeding, and to control pain.

I immediately demanded the bleeding to stop, and you know what, it did. At this point the medical doctor would claim, and rightly so, that our body has a survival mechanism that triggers and aids us to respond to survive. I agree. But when one possesses a powerful imagination along with fear, it overrides any physiological response that would react, and one can (and many times does) bleed to death, or die of shock caused from fear and panic. I could have been one of those statistics had it not been for the SILVA METHOD techniques to stop the bleeding.

After thirty-five minutes of lying in the car seat until help arrived, I was placed in an ambulance which sirened all the way to the hospital's emergency receiving unit. I questioned why the BIG RUSH, for the events that followed were a farce.

After being wheeled into the emergency room for incoming patients, I lay on a cold table for an hour or more, while papers had to be signed, and until my turn came for a "look at." I kept my eyes closed, since the flood lights I was directly under were intense. Finally, two staff members came to view my broken body. One had this to say, "I wonder what she looked like?"

I tell you this not to belittle the hospital system,

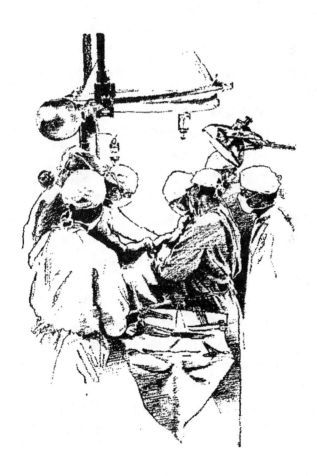

because I'm sure the staff only do what they know. I hope this will help you handle a situation if you ever happen to be in a similar circumstance. I hope you never are.

Again I had a chance to feel sorry for myself, rant, rave, moan, and groan, or control the situation by thinking positive (another supreme test). So I began my mental musings with constructive, creative thinking. "I will be fine; why, with the remarkable plastic surgery I hear they are now doing, I know they can improve on my looks. This body will heal itself so fast, my medical case history will be a miracle for its speedy recovery." Over and over I mentally told myself the above positive suggestions.

The diagnosis of the injuries sustained from the accident after a complete once-over, twice-over, three times-over (I must say once they got around to examining me, they were most thorough) were: fractured ribs in the lower back, bruised spleen, right ankle swollen three times the normal size. They could find no reason for this as there was no fracture visible in X-ray. Immediate surgery to reconstruct my nose and repair facial damage was recommended. I was given sodium pentathol to undergo face and nose surgery.

Prognosis for the damage and injury in the back, ribs, and ankle would be six weeks of limited activity in a wheelchair, plus wearing a corset for back support.

After the facial surgery, and upon regaining consciousness, I woke up to a room full of friends who came to bring healing energy. People truly are

beautiful. One of my friends, a former registered nurse, insisted on just sitting beside my bed as she claimed she could sense my physical needs. She would administer to my needs until the anesthetic wore completely off, and I was in control and rational.

After my system was free of the drugs administered for surgery, I never had another shot or pain-killing pill during the two weeks I remained in the hospital. I didn't need it. When I was aware of discomfort, I merely "conned" myself by imagining the throbs of pain (that I was once so fearful of) were healing pulsations. With each awareness of the throbbing sensation, I mentally repeated, "Healing, healing, healing."

This is interesting, for this was the first time I realized the throbbing sensation, that is called pain comes in cycles, and isn't constant. I also was aware that when I used the technique of physical relaxation, which I was taught in the Silva Class the intensity of the throbbing was very mild. I now had changed pain cycles to positive healing cycles; there was no more pain, only pleasant healing pulsations.

Ah ha, I sense doubt in some of you readers. This is to be expected, for prior to my Mind (Control) Development training; I too, had been a big doubter. Some of you might call this technique self-hypnosis, programming, or plain stupidity, since drugs were available to keep me knocked out. But I will say, not one of you can say it doesn't work, because I'm here

116

to tell you it did and it does.

I must keep telling you the power of the mind is fantastic. I'm sure some of you are aware of the firewalkers who walk over hot coals and do not get burned, nor do they feel discomfort; or of the people that are human pin-cushions and feel no pain as pins are stuck in their bodies. They have conditioned and disciplined themselves with their thinking to such a degree, that they actually refuse pain. They are not special people. I certainly am not special. We all have this ability to control feelings, pain, our environments and our lives. Don't limit yourself for this works in all capacities.

BIG QUESTION MARK: "But I haven't had any mental training, so how does one develop this powerful, positive attitude you're talking about?" In "Chapter Nine," I will give you a step-by-step plan for positive thinking results. But remember, you must first have the desire to be master of your mind.

Scientists tell us that we are using less than ten per cent of our mind power. I believe it, because, as I continue to study mind power, I am amazed at what one is capable of doing by right or by wrong thinking.

My healing was what one might term a "miracle." When I was released from the hospital, and back at home, the wheelchair came right home with me. Of course it served a useful purpose. I looked at it as it sat in the corner, while I took over my household activities. I thought, "I am not an invalid. I am in complete control of my body. My body does not control me. I control my body." And boy, did it straighten up and perform!

I was requested to check with the doctor who did the face surgery, and the doctor who was tending to my back and leg injury. I really didn't want to go, but it was required by the doctors for other reports to collect fees from the accident insurance company.

I first went to the surgeon who did such a fine job of rebuilding my nose. He was about to probe and "nose around," and check his workmanship by inserting a metal object up my nose, when I rebelled. I told him I was quite happy with my nose job. I felt great. It had healed perfectly, and I had no further need for wasting his time or my time. Yes, I was rude and I'm sure I hurt his pride by being so abrupt.

My policy to always "leave 'em laughing, loving, loyal, and lucky to know me" was a BUST. I goofed miserably, so I had no choice but to make amends.

I have always been proud of having a sense of humor (although sometimes my husband disagrees with me and tells me that my humor doesn't make sense). Nevertheless, I spent the next day trying to compensate for my rude behavior during my visit to the good doctor. I hoped that he might have a sense of humor, so I pulled out my crayons. (I keep them on hand for my grandchildren when they come for a "getting into everything" session.) I drew a beautiful picture of my nose. I then composed a citation which I typed and attached under the drawing of the nose. I then framed the entire masterpiece, and titled it: AWARD OF MERIT FOR DR. (and inserted his name). The citation read as follows: "After extensive nosin' around and getting this thing back in runnin' condition, I am most appreciative. You have not only performed a humanitarian duty, you have definitely improved upon my beauty. All that now remains is paying through it." Then I signed my name.

Perhaps my husband was right when he said my sense of humor sometimes doesn't make sense, for I promptly received a bill for his services, and I haven't seen or heard from the dear boy since. To the readers who are inclined to agree with my husband's view that my humor doesn't make sense, that's fine. But give me credit on this score—I may be a nut, but you can bet I'll never be in a rut.

Contesting: The Name It and Claim It Game

Chapter Nine

WINeuvers For WISHcraft

Contesting: The Name It and Claim It Game

WINeuvers
For
WISHcraft

"I knew I was going to win," said the winner of a $10,000, first-prize, cash award.

So the news came as no surprise when the Dallas woman answered her doorbell, and two representatives of an advertising agency were there to present her with a check for $10,000.

The story began last Summer when the woman told two of her best friends, 'This is going to be my year. My whole life is going to change. I feel it, I KNOW it."

Just what did she do to accomplish this *WIN-fall?* Why she used her power of positive thinking.

In her words, she summed it up this way. "If you just open your heart and believe in good things, they are bound to happen. You simply train your mind to believe and to hope until it happens."

Her goal was not for $10,000. Actually it was for $5,000. She also had three things she wanted to accomplish for the year.

"I needed a new car; I wanted to establish a home again with a good husband; I play the organ at my church, but I never owned one of my own, and have always wanted one so I could play at home; and lastly, I wanted a little, financial security, and felt that $5,000 would be ample," she related.

"I made a 'wheel of fortune,' a simple circular piece of cardboard with cut-out pictures tacked to it. There were pictures of a new automobile, a couple holding hands (depicting happiness), an electric organ, and a nest with an egg representing the $5,000:I boldly printed the sum of $5,000 on the egg. I put the wheels (because I actually made four) in places where I would be constantly reminded of my goals, and could give them energy continuously. All that remained was for them to materialize," she laughed.

124

Chapter Nine

One of her wheels of fortune was placed on her TV; another on the dash of her car; the other in her desk drawer at work; and the other on her night stand, as they would be the last thing she could think about before falling asleep.

With all those reminders, it was a constant process of sending energy out. It's a good idea because that's better than thinking of aches and pains, or feeling sorry for yourself. In some schools of thought it is called being "single-minded." Within a few weeks, she was able to buy a new car. "It was a deal I couldn't turn down. Why it was almost like a gift," she explained. She then removed the picture of the car from her wheel of fortune.

For one of the church programs, a traveling gospel quartet presented the program. She was attracted to one of the members, and they found they had a lot in common. Several months later, he returned to Dallas, left the quartet, took a job locally, and they got married. Another picture was removed.

It was in May on her birthday, when her husband presented her with an organ for their home. Three down, one to go.

"He knew of my projects. In fact, he got a kick out of it. But he said, 'Okay, kid, I got two for you, but I can't imagine how, or where you will get a lump sum of $5,000.'"

125

Contesting: The Name It and Claim It Game

"It was the second week in June when I was notified I won not $5,000, but the first prize of $10,000 in a sweepstake. I'd seen the ad of the contest in a magazine and mailed it in. I told myself at the time, here is where I can get my egg money."

All her dreams were realized within a year. The beauty of this true story is, we all have the capability, so let's discuss how one can accomplish this, and how it works.

Do you know what you really want? Don't be too quick with your answer because the average person has so many wants, desires, and wishes. They change daily with one's moods. You are not able to give yourself the chance to generate enough energy for your end result if you vacillate.

I suggest you play this mental game with yourself. Ask yourself, "What is the most important goal I wish to accomplish?" Think about it seriously. Is it positive, constructive, and creative? Sort of imagine having it. Feel how it feels to have it. How will it change your lifestyle?

A word of advice. You need never involve another to obtain your end result. Imposing your will on others in a NO-NO and is really not necessary. Let me give you this example. You are working in an office position. Your boss is a fink, he goofs off and there is only one way to do things, his way. You feel

126

he lacks the knowledge for this position, and you know you would like the money that job offers. You want his job. You might entertain the idea that he gets fired, or the higher boss gets wise to him as you have, and at last, you get the position you should have had all along. Granted, we all fantasize this type of situation at times. We dismiss it because our mind gets busy on other things.

What I'm saying is, if you kept up this thought long enough and strong enough for it to become an obsession, chances are that it would happen in due time. THIS IS NOT THE WAY TO PLAY THE GAME. You can obtain the same end results with peace of mind and not have to manipulate people. You can enjoy your achievements with this method: "I desire the perfect job with perfect pay." That is all that is necessary. Every time your job comes to mind, repeat this phrase silently, or think about it. With this as an end result, it will work its way to fruition in due course. Your boss may be transferred, resign, or whatever, or you may even be offered another job with another firm that may meet all your needs. There is no need to set things up, just watch how they all fall into place. For if this is truly your end result, and you use proper mental desire, you will accomplish it.

One of the finest publications that goes into

detail on a plan to accomplish a goal is titled, *IT WORKS*, by R.H.J., published by Scrivener and Co., and distributed by DeVorss and Co., P.O. Box 550, Marina del Rey, California 90291.

As I lecture throughout the United States, I get questions from the audience in regard to particular situations. I also ask them if they wish to write and tell me their experiences of how they obtained their end result. The following is an incident that happened to a student.

"But I don't enter contests, and I don't feel that I can afford the money out of the family budget for my desire," she said.

Her desire was to take a trip to the Bahamas Seems like one of her friends had taken the leisure cruise and had related how great it was. It so impressed the student that she too, wanted to make the voyage. Her husband, however, did not share her enthusiasm, nor did he care to go. That did not dampen her desire. She still wanted it for herself.

I suggested she continue to project energy, and know that her wish would come true.

Four weeks later is when I received the post card with a picture of a ship, postmarked from the Bahamas. The card merely stated, "I named it and am now claiming it," and her signature.

Upon her return home she wrote me the

details of how this all came about. While taking art classes she got acquainted with one of the other students in her class. The student, who was a distributor for women's cosmetics, told the lady that the company she worked for was having a sales promotion, and the person in each district with the largest sales would win a trip to the Bahamas. She was confident she would win the trip. To date, she had submitted the largest amount of sales. That is when the student told her of her desire to take such a trip. The lady wished her artist friend success on her win and hoped that her trip would be all she had dreamed.

A week later, she received a phone call from the artist friend. She had won the trip and was ready to leave when her son suddenly became ill and had to undergo an appendectomy. She couldn't leave under these conditions, and she knew of no one in her family that could make or want the trip on such short notice. If it was not taken, it would be lost as it was a preplanned, package deal. So, if she wanted the trip, it was hers free with no strings attached. Of course, she accepted and was elated because the experience was everything she had hoped for. She confessed that she was amazed how quickly everything fell into place.

Recently I met a woman in one of the shopping centers in Dallas who recognized me. She heard my lecture on "WINeuvers for WISHcraft" and immediately applied the ideas. She had to share her success. She and her husband had just moved into a new home and were in the process of furnishing it. After hearing my lecture, she knew what her desire would be. She wanted a china cabinet just like her grandmother had. She recalled how she admired the piece of furniture whenever she visited her. When her grandmother passed away, her estate was sold and distributed, and no one seemed to know just where the china cabinet was now. Nevertheless, her desire was to have the china cabinet or a duplicate, placed against one wall in her breakfast area.

Several weeks later, a friend asked her to accompany her to an antique store. She went and there was the china cabinet. If it was not the original, the one owned by her grandmother, it certainly was its twin. There was no difference. She was delighted until she heard the cost.

"But that didn't deflate me, and I didn't entertain any doubt that I would have it," she assured me. "I told my husband about it and he went to look at it He agreed it certainly would be perfect for our breakfast area, but at this time, our budget could not handle it. We left the store, and on the way home my husband carefully explained the many reasons why we could not afford it. I listened and said nothing. I can honestly tell you I did not mention the china cabinet again. I merely knew it was mine, and visualized it standing against the bare wall."

'Two months later when a delivery truck backed into our driveway, I thought they had the wrong house," she continued. 'The man that rang the doorbell asked me where I wanted the china cabinet placed. Shortly later, when my husband arrived home, he found me in tears, as I was stroking the beautiful carvings on my polished, china cabinet. He too, knew it was mine and found no problem paying for it. He told me that the day he chose to go back and look at it again, in hopes he could get it at a reduced price, he found to his delight, that it had been marked down to half price. The store was in the process of moving to a new location, and had reduced all their merchandise for quick removal."

Some of you might be saying, 'That's not so great. I always get what I'm after when I nag long enough." Another might think, "My, what an unusual husband she has. Mine would be too tight." Still otters may not even want an antique china cabinet.

The moral of this story: No naggin'; no negative thinking that the price made it unobtainable; just steady, positive energy and a knowing it would be china cabinet.

I have to admire this beautiful, positive attitude, because she then told me she was working on another major goal that she would materialize soon.

What is your pleasure? Don't just sit there.

SELECT IT. PROJECT IT. EXPECT IT.

Chapter Nine

Contesting: The Name It and Claim It Game

PART
TWO OF
THE NAME IT
AND CLAIM IT GAME

(WITH MORE
WINEUVERS FOR WISHCRAFT)

Contesting: The Name It and Claim It Game

EIGHT
YEARS
LATER

The second part of this book is a step-by-step guide to entering contests to win as a fun and profitable hobby. It provides technical know-how, and specific action to take toward acquiring your goals. It lists how to set up your contest files and keep records.

The portions of my daily diary of personal experiences will be shared honestly and accurately, and should prove to be most helpful and simple to understand.

Contesting: The Name It and Claim It Game

I will make no statement or guarantee that you will be a consistent winner. I can only share with you what I did and what results I accomplished. Is it worth the time and postage money for you? You must decide.

I still receive letters from people who read the first part of this book and benefited from my suggestions. It is truly nice to hear from you and about your wins. More power to you.

"What have you won lately?" still seems to be the opening statements by many that write to me, or by people I meet when I lecture. To answer the questions, yes, we are still living in and enjoying the dream home we won some years ago.

A new interest sparked for me, after the house win: Power of the Mind, Self-hypnosis, Silva Mind Development, and "Self-I-Wareness."

I have studied all courses and programs, here and abroad, on these subjects. I wanted to understand "me" better. During my active traveling and lecturing from coast to coast, I no longer had the time or interest to enter sweepstakes and creative writing contests.

One June, several years ago, Pat, my husband, retired from his "8-to-5" job. I reached another decision to stay home and write fulltime. I'd met so many, exciting, interesting people during my lecturing and traveling, I wanted to write and tell others how they solved their problems and projects with a positive attitude. I began typing and getting it on paper from the notes I gathered. I am still compiling the information. I also decided to, once again, contest for the fun of it.

I started sending entries that same month my husband retired, just to get back in the swing of it. I did not keep a record of my daily activities, or how many entries I submitted. I did, however, keep a record of what I had won from that June to December period. The following is what I won a: travel clock, toy, Schaeffer pen set, leather belt, billfold with $100 check, gold money clip, check for $1,000, check for $30, canvas bag, personalized coffee mug, and a check for $25.

Beginning in January, I kept a daily calendar-diary of my entries sent, postage, time I allotted, and items won.

I feel anyone can relate to this "at-a-glance" record, and perhaps may wish to use the guidelines for their contesting.

May you reap the rewards, pleasure, and success that I continue to find in this exciting hobby of entering contests to WIN.

Helen Hadsell

Contesting: The Name It and Claim It Game

Chapter Ten

Keys
To
Winning

Contesting: The Name It and Claim It Game

Keys
To
Winning

HOW MANY OF YOU HAVE VISIONS OF OPENING A LETTER ONE DAY AND FINDING A CHECK FOR $100,000; A PHONE CALL TELLING YOU YOU JUST WON IN THE "READER'S DIGEST" PROMOTIONAL SWEEPSTAKES IN - PUBLISHER'S CLEARING HOUSE," OR ANY OF THE OTHER SWEEPSTAKES THAT ARE GOING ON TODAY? SOMEBODY WINS. WHY NOT YOU? ARE THEY JUST LUCKY? DO THEY KNOW THE JUDGING AGENCY, THE DIRECTOR, OR THE

Contesting: The Name It and Claim It Game

SPONSOR? WHAT IS THE CATCH; THE SECRET OF
BEING A CONSISTENT WINNER?

Winning big in sweepstakes, creative writing
contests, or lotteries may be fantasies to some, but to
more and more people these dreams are becoming
reality. In the past, it was the woman who entered
contests and won most prizes. Housebound with small
children, limited in experience or education, she
dreamed of all the extras that could be obtained by
entering contests. She won because her desire was so
intense, she mentally made it happen. "WISHING
WILL MAKE IT SO" is not fiction, it is fact
Today, more and more men's names are
appearing on winners' lists, and they are capturing
some of the big prizes, especially in recipe contests. In a
local recipe contest recently sponsored by a
newspaper, twenty prizes were offered. The four, top
winners were men, the ladies only captured eight of the
prizes, and the rest of the prizes were awarded to men.
At the present time our area supermarkets are
distributing Bingo tickets with each store visit
'The men are making more trips to purchase one
item to get the tickets than women are," said several
grocery checkers when I asked what the response
was.

So what does that tell us? Why, that just about everyone likes the idea of taking a chance, buying a ticket, sending in an entry to a sweepstakes contest so they can be declared a WINNER.

WHY NOT?

Anyone can get on the BRAND WAGON and cook with an AMANA RADARANGE, sew on a SINGER, fly via BRANIFF or AMERICAN to that special place. I call it the "NAME IT AND CLAIM IT GAME," because that is exactly what I have been doing, off and on, for the past twenty years.

Whether it's lotteries, Bingo tickets, mailing entries, checking numbers, or registering for door prizes, it's FUN. It's EXCITING being a WINNER.

Unfortunately, not everyone wins. If you have ever kept a track record of winners, be it in sports, art, literature, acting, and yes, even in contesting, you will find that most of the people win consistently. The same names appear on top of the winner's list. So what is their secret?

I've read enough of their comments, and listened to their interviews to realize there is a common denominator with winners:

1. They decide what they want.

Contesting: The Name It and Claim It Game

2. They imagine they have it.
3. They KNOW they will get it.

Chapter Ten

Contesting: The Name It and Claim It Game

Chapter Eleven

How The Right Attitude Makes A Winner

Contesting: The Name It and Claim It Game

How The Right Attitude Makes A Winner

Deciding what you want, imagining you have it, and KNOWING it will be yours are the KEYS to being a winner. There is another attribute that is obvious with most of the winners: their attitude.

"You are what you think." I'm sure you are all familiar with that phrase. In the past (now just stop and think for a minute), did you have good luck? Get the job you wanted? Did you ever win anything in a raffle, at Bingo, or at the races? Was it consistent, or

are you a BORN LOSER? Nothing ever went right. Somebody else always wins. Chances on lotteries or postage spent on sweepstakes was a waste of time and money.

Now give it some thought. How was your attitude? Was it like ninety per cent of people? 'The idea seemed like a good one at the time. I wanted to win because heaven knows I could use the money."

Did you harbor guilt feelings about winning? Many times this comes from our religious background: "I shouldn't ask for material things. That's a sin."

YOU ARE WHAT YOU THINK, remember. It shouldn't take you too long now to realize that what you thought in the past you actually are now.

"Okay, I'll buy that," you may now agree. "So how do I go about changing my thinking, my attitude, and my luck to become a winner?" The answer is: THINK IT, DO IT, BECOME IT.

The first step is so simple you may overlook it, until you discipline yourself to become aware of what you think. Although this book is slanted toward being a winner in contests, you and I both know that LIFE IS A GAME. We can play the game to be a winner.

When you apply the following principles, they will carry over to all facets of your life; your job, marriage, health, and wealth.

Begin today to become aware of your thinking. In the past, if you thought, "Not me," change it to, "Why not me?" Change the phrase, "I can't" to "I can."

Today is a new day and a new beginning. Anything you thought or spoke about in the past that meant doubt, failure, or was of a negative nature is gone and buried. You need no longer dwell in the past, nor need you identify with any hardship, heartache, or heartbreak you experienced. Realize you are a POWERFUL person.

Every thought you harbor in fear, anger, or pain seems to accumulate more energy, and it will eventually become reality. "Hang in there long enough and strong enough, and you will get it," is a cosmic law. 'There are no failures, only delays in results," also applies here. How long it takes to manifest depends on the energy and thought directed to it.

Would it not make sense for you to achieve a healthy, wealthy, successful, winner's attitude in all areas? You MUST now think in a constructive, positive way.

I AM A WINNER. I WILL ACHIEVE ALL MY GOALS.

Contesting: The Name It and Claim It Game

Chapter Twelve

What Do You Want?

Contesting: The Name It and Claim It Game

What Do You Want?

What do you wish to achieve? What is your desire? Let's find out and get on with living, loving, and learning in the classroom of life, where the MEEK shall inherit the earth only if they have the DESIRE.

ACQUIRE A DESIRE TO WIN WHAT?

You already have a desire to be a winner or you wouldn't be reading this book. But what is it you

.

Contesting: The Name It and Claim It Game

want to win in the contest game? Is it a new car, a trip, money, a home, a boat, a skateboard? What?

Some of the following suggestions were given by students that attended my classes (not necessarily available from contests).

BETTER JOB ... BETTER LIFE LOTS
OF MONEY ... SEXY WIFE

FOREIGN CAR ... PRIVATE PLANE
NAME IN LIGHTS ... CLAIM TO FAME

ROCKING CHAIR... COLOR TV PLACE
IN COUNTRY ... SECURITY

I WANT TO WIN THE FOOTBALL POOL, AND
SIT BACK WHILE OTHERS DROOL

FIFTY THOUSAND WOULD SURE BE NEAT
I'D INVEST, YOU GUESSED, I'D BE ON EASY
STREET

WHO ME? ALL I WANT IS PEACE-
POWER-PERFECTION

MAKE MINE...
KNOWLEDGE... WISDOM... UNDERSTANDING

What does the five-year-old, neighbor girl want? Why all she wants is a handful of bubble gum—NOW. She wants to make the bubble as big as her friend, Cindy. One that will cover her entire face. (It so happened I had a pound package of bubble gum on hand. I'm a bubble blower, too.) She had her desire immediately.

Some of our desires may take a bit longer to set things in motion. Bear in mind, *THERE ARE NEVER ANY FAILURES, ONLY DELAYS IN RESULTS.*

Once, on a New Year's Day, I made a list of things I wanted to win in the sweepstake and contest games of that coming year.

1. A microwave oven. I have one I use daily in my kitchen. I found it to be so handy and time-saving, I also wanted one for our lake cabin.

2. A new car. A gas saver. I had never won a car up to then, and I thought it would be a good project to aim at. I even got specific and made it white with blue upholstery.

3. A trip to Hawaii. No, I've never been to Hawaii. Sure, I've been to Europe six times, even to Russia, and the interior of Mexico several times, but not Hawaii, not yet!

4. Any other wins, I wanted cash. That's a BIG

ORDER, you may think. I look at it as being a lot of fun. How long will it take to accomplish these goals? When I have projected enough energy to make them reality, and I have visualized having them, until I have accomplished my goals.

Perhaps you may want to start with one item. Okay, it's your show, so get in the act.

I feel the more one thinks and visualizes his goals and desires, the more energy is directed to the project, and the sooner it can be accomplished. In order to make it a daily reminder, I took a 5" x 7" card, and with a marks-a-lot, I printed in bold letters, MICROWAVE OVEN. CAR. HAWAII. MONEY.

I taped it to the dash of my little ol' Hornet I drove and had planned to replace. I taped another card saying the same thing on the bookrack which sits on my desk. This simply reminded me to give my projects energy by thinking about them. Every time I read the cards, I brief ly closed my eyes (only takes twenty to thirty seconds), and saw the microwave oven sitting in the corner of my kitchen counter out at our lake cabin. This was just imagining that I had it there already.

I had my husband measure the space it required, and asked him to extend the counter to accommodate the oven so it would be ready when I won it. He did it one morning. He even found the same counter finish that matched the existing counter, and it was ready. My husband is my greatest *"Winspiration."* He not only encourages me in all I my ventures, but he projects the end-result image for me, too.

It was January 1st when I began to project for a microwave oven. It was February 22nd when I I received the phone call from the local representative of the Rath Meat Company. He told me I had won an Amana Radarange for the winning recipe I submitted in their recipe contest.

I scratched MICROWAVE OVEN off my list and began concentrating on the car, Hawaii, and money prizes.

My car end-result picture was me sitting behind the wheel of a white car with blue upholstery. My imagination got so vivid, I was beginning to smell the newness of the interior. When I thought of my trip to Hawaii, I pictured my husband and me walking on the beach. We both had on bathing suits, and it was warm and sunny.

Contesting: The Name It and Claim It Game

Chapter Thirteen

The Difference Between Desire and Knowing

Contesting: The Name It and Claim It Game

The Difference
Between Desire
and Knowing

It was Sunday, March 27, when I spotted the full-page ad in the Dallas paper announcing that a local radio station, KLIF, and the local area Datsun dealers were giving away twelve Datsuns, two a week for the next six weeks. Ah ha, I thought, an opportunity to get my car.

Requirements were to register at a local dealer, or mail in a card to the radio station. Rules stated there would be a drawing of all entries received. The radio personality (D.J. to me) would make the calls and ask the question, "What is your favorite radio station?" Your answer, to be a winner, would be "KLIF 1190 is my favorite radio station." A week after the close of the contest the twelve win-ners would gather at a local showroom, and there would be a drawing of keys to find out which Datsun you won. Would it be a Lil' Hustler, a B-210, an F-10 Sports Wagon, or a Honeybee?

After reading the ad, I got so excited I didn't bother reading the rest of the paper at that time. I went to my desk immediately. The contest was to begin Monday, which was the very next day, so I wanted to get some entries in the first day, because chances would be better with fewer entries. In a contest where drawings are held over a period of time, it's best to get in on the first of it, then continue to send in one or more entries each day until your name is called. By 2 PM Sunday, I had mailed four cards.

Copying a sample entry blank, pictured in the ad, I used colored poster board and cut out cards in the shape of the car pictured in the newspaper ad. The time spent doing it added positive energy to my goal. It takes a little effort on your part to set up the situation for yourself, but it's fun being creative.

I venture to say, hundreds of thousands of

166

people noticed the full-page ad, and I'm sure many found it interesting and had a desire to win one of the cars; Some would put the ad aside to give it further study; and some would actually cut out the blank and mail it, which would be the first step. It takes one more step to be a winner: to picture yourself having the car or being in the car, or whatever your creative imagination comes up with.

Monday morning began fun-and-game time for me; waiting to get the phone call so I would be a car winner. Fortunately, the station plays country & western and I really dig it. You really didn't have to listen to the radio all day. You simply had to answer correctly when they called. In order not to goof when they called, perhaps forget to mention 1190 and lose out, I placed a card beside the phones throughout the house. Each one said, "When a D.J. calls and asks you what your favorite radio station is, this is what you answer (exactly): 'KLIF 1190 is my favorite radio station.'" This was also for my husband's use in case they called when I wasn't home.

About two o'clock on Monday they announced the first winner, a girl in Dallas. One down, eleven to go. "Which one will I be?" I asked myself. On Friday they called a man in Ft. Worth, and he gave the correct answer, In the meantime, I mailed in one entry each day. I also made a trip to the Datsun put my name in their hopper. The following week! listened whenever I was home. I realized then they called people on Monday and Friday. Monday they announced another winner. That left nine cars.

It was Friday, April 8 when I woke up and KNEW I would win a car today.

At this point, let me define the difference between DESIRE and KNOWING. DESIRE IS EXCITED ANTICIPATION, KNOWING IS CALM ASSURANCE. For example: You are present at a drawing and your first three numbers are called. You feel like you are about to explode. The last number is called and you missed by one number. This is a DESIRE feeling and very common. You have re- pressed energy and you are wanting it to happen. Unfortunately, there has not been enough energy projected to make it so at that time.

When you KNOW something, it is a different feeling. You have a calm, cool assurance; all anxiety is gone; it is already done. All that now remains is to experience the physical presentation. BEING CALM AND COOL WHEN YOU COLLECT. It is a good feeling.

Become aware of this KNOWING feeling in all areas of your life, and you are well on your way to total "I-wareness."

Chapter Thirteen

It's not negative to KNOW you're not going to win at something sometimes. It just lets you KNOW that enough energy has not been projected to make it reality.

You can play games and kid yourself by quitting your job because you have the DESIRE to win a $100,000 prize. Until you know the difference between DESIRE and KNOWING, don't be foolhardy. Keep your job. One day you will know the difference with I-wareness.

Several years ago I gave a lecture to a group of business women at a convention in Fort Worth. The literature that was mailed out to the membership about my being the speaker, must have impressed one of the women. She approached me just before the program began, and told me her desire. Tomorrow night, the last night of the convention, they would have a drawing for a door prize. The prize was an ocean cruise. "I want it so bad I can taste the salt water," she said.

"My husband and I are having problems, and I feel if we have this time together, we can work it out," she continued. "I know if you project enough energy for me to win this cruise, I will get it," she concluded. She gave a sigh, and a calmness came over her.

"You already have the cruise," I assured her. Tomorrow night when they have the drawing and call your name, act surprised. They expect you to." For a moment, she thought I was jesting, then she said with enthusiasm, "I'll call and tell you."

Shortly after eight o'clock the following night, she called. "I won. I KNEW I would after I talked to

you, but how did you know?" she asked.

"Do you recall when you sighed as if a great burden had been lifted off your shoulders?" I asked.

"Why yes" she said. "I was so relieved that I

got to talk to you before the program. I was concerned someone might get to you first and ask you to help them win," she explained.

As a matter of fact, someone else had approached me earlier and asked for my help to win. I did. She obviously didn't want this particular cruise. That's not to say she will never take or win a cruise. It only means at this time, there wasn't enough energy projected by her to make it happen. If it remains important to her, she should continue to give it energy until she is actually on the ship. The majority of people never complete their goals. They jump to something else.

A number of years ago I had a dream, and it was a "lulu." I was in a great hall that was packed with merchandise. There were cars, boats, clothes, furniture, appliances, and TV's. There was a man standing at the door as if waiting. I asked who all this merchandise belonged to. His answer was, 'This is the place where people's dreams are stored. Trouble is, they give up and release the energy too soon, so I keep them in storage. Once in a while some of them get back to it and claim their dreams."

Do any of you have something stored in that room? Don't be flighty. If you have a goal or desire, hang in until you get it. Also, I must advise you, make sure you want it before you send out all that good energy.

Before concluding our conversation, I told the cruise winner that if her marriage was as important to her as the winning of that trip, I was certain that she could solve that problem, cruise or not.

Projecting energy toward any goal, with steady determination, will eventually be fruitful. This applies to any situation.

In contesting, it makes it doubly exciting when you get the KNOWING feeling, because it means you have succeeded in your project, and it's time for making another goal. A wise man once said, *'The three things in life that make it worthwhile are: to feel useful by doing something, to be loved by someone, to have something to look forward to."*

It was shortly after four o'clock on the day I KNEW I was going to win my car. The phone rang. It was my husband. He was fixing the plumbing at our rental house. He had broken a pipe, and wanted me to go to the plumber for a fitting. I didn't want to go because I wanted to be home when the radio station called to tell me I was their fourth, Datsun winner. I might call this "the supreme test with self," I was so sure I would win, I told myself they would only call after I got back home, since it would take less than half an hour. I left. It was the Friday before Easter and many of the shops closed early. I had to go from hardware store to hardware store. I finally found the fitting and took it to my husband. When I got back home it was after 6 PM. I turned on the radio and the D.J. just announced that they now had four winners and would call the people again Monday. I couldn't believe it. How had I missed? I was so sure my KNOWING feeling was right.

The phone rang. It was my oldest son. He had an apartment on the other side of town and came over occasionally for a free meal or to check to see if he has any mail.

"Hey mom, I won a Datsun about an hour ago," he calmly announced. He had come by to check the mail. The phone rang. Someone asked to speak to me. He told them I wasn't there, but could he help, or take a message. "Why yes you can. What is your favorite radio station?"

"For a second I was off guard," he told me. "I then saw the card taped to the phone and knew what It was all about. So I answered, 'KLIF 1190 is her favorite radio station.'"

"Your mom will be proud of you tonight. You just won her a new Datsun," he announced.

Later I heard the taped call when they played back the conversation with my son. Big question: Would I have won that Friday had my son not been there to answer the phone? As I listened the week

173

earlier, several times when they made calls and there was no answer, they drew another name. Was my son supposed to be there at that time to make it possible? I don't have the answer. I just KNEW I would win that day.

When all twelve winners were drawn, we all gathered at the showroom to draw for our keys to one of the twelve cars. There was no white car with blue upholstery. Instead, I won a blue, Datsun, pick-up truck. That certainly was not the car I had projected.

To me that was not the end result. I put an ad in the paper the following week and sold it. This win turned out to be MONEY.

Sure I could have gone out and bought a car, the one I wanted with the money I received for selling the truck, but that's not the way I wanted it. There was still a white car with blue upholstery out there for me to WIN.

The rest of that year, I won minor, merchandise prizes, and a number of cash prizes. Yes, enough to buy my car and take a trip to Hawaii. That wouldn't be fun though. I had the patience to continue to project energy until I got the phone call telling me of a Hawaii trip, a car, or big money prize wins.

Someone once said it takes patience, persistence, and postage to be a contest winner. I agree with that statement, but I believe the thing that makes It happen is the energy you direct toward it. Don't rely on LUCK. LUCK is like a rubber crutch: it will let you *down* when you try to lean on it.

MAKE IT HAPPEN. Decide what you want. Help it along by giving it energy for your end-result accomplishment.

Entering contests is an excellent avenue to pursue, because it offers the material things you should have been accustomed to a long time ago.

Contesting: The Name It and Claim It Game

Chapter Fourteen

Supplies For The Contester

Contesting: The Name It and Claim It Game

Supplies For
The
Contester

In the contesting business, like any other, a penny saved is a penny earned. Supplies make up a large chunk of the cost, and are, therefore, a target for economy.

Keep The Following Rules In Mind For Buying Envelopes:

1. Check both office supply and discount stores for sales.

2. The unit prices are significantly lower when you buy larger quantities at the same time.

3. If space for storing supplies is limited, you can share larger purchases with other customers.

4. Don't overlook the economy of re-using envelopes you receive. If they haven't been marked up too badly, you might paste colorful tape or use a colored pencil to cover up the return address.

5. Call or visit the local print shops. Many times they are overstocked, or envelopes become misprinted and are rejected. You can get them at a low cost and cover up the printing with a stick-on-slogan, or a Marks-a-lot pen, or whatever.

6. Envelope size or color in most instances, does not matter when entering a sweepstakes. Many times contest rules state that only a #10 (9 1/2" x 4 1/8) or smaller size envelope can be submitted. FOLLOW THE RULES TO THE LETTER.

Pens And Pencils

Pens and pencils are cheaper in large quantities. Do keep a good supply of colored pens on hand. It's easier to write with them, and it breaks the monotony of using the same color.

Paper And Cards

Most rules call for submitting your name on a 3" x 5" piece of paper. In that case, any type of paper is permissible. Again, I suggest you make friends with print shops. They sometimes have test copies and overruns they cannot use. Business offices often discard the old letterhead stationery or revised forms. Ask friends that work in offices, as that is a source you might benefit from. Any color or weight of paper is fine.

Some rules state to print your name on a 3" x 5" card. If this is their request, then by all means use a card. The index cards can be purchased at any discount store. Perhaps you have an unclaimed freight store in your area. That too, is a good source for less expensive, paper products.

One of my contesting friends gets her paper from the newspaper printing dock. They usually have roll ends available that they discard. She has a paper cutter and always has a good supply of 3 x 5's on hand. She is also generous, and we all benefit from her supply. FREE IS MUCH BETTER THAN CHEAP.

How To Keep A Record Of Contesting Activities

I keep a detailed record of contest activities on a giant-size calendar I buy for around one dollar. Each day, as I take my envelopes out of the file box, I count the stamps I stick on and make a note of how many I send. I also make a note of how much time I allotted to signing my name or addressing envelopes.

Write down every penny spent on paper, envelopes, and stamps. That is part of expenses and can be deducted at the end of the year for income tax records. Be sure to write a check or get a receipt from the post office for the stamps purchased. This is your biggest expense. Don't begrudge the postage money spent. When I stamp my envelopes before I mail them off, I mentally project positive energy to each envelope by thinking: "HERE GOES ANOTHER WINNER THAT WILL BRING ME BACK MY END RESULT."

Don't be like the woman I once had as a neighbor. One evening she called and asked if she could drive to the post office with me. (We talked earlier over the fence, and she knew I was going to make the trip later.) She entered contests halfheartedly, because she knew I kept winning things. When we reached the Post Office, she leaned out to deposit our entries in the curb letter box. As she slipped them in the slot, she turned to me and said, "Well there goes nothing." I was dumbfounded. She never did win anything while I knew her. Later she moved out of the neighborhood, and took her gloom with her.

We all have "down" periods occasionally. If it is a constant thing, it really is the pits. If this happens to you, make a considerable effort to get back into a positive frame of mind. Read something uplifting; listen to violin music—it is the most uplifting, soothing sound one can experience. Remember, you are in control of your thinking. Change if it's pulling you down.

Contesting: The Name It and Claim It Game

Chapter Fifteen

The Steps I Take To Enter Contests

Contesting: The Name It and Claim It Game

The Steps I Take To Enter Contests

The following is an example of a contest I had entered. Please note: Rules state entries must be postmarked by October 17. For a postmark deadline of October 17, I mailed in my last entry on the 13th or 14th of October to be safe.

SAFEGUARD'S SMALLEST SOAPSTAKES. GRAND PRIZE: (1) A 2-week trip for two to the smallest countries in Europe—Monaco, The Vatican, Liechtenstein, Luxembourg, etc. worth $5,000, or a cash alternate of $5,000. **FIRST PRIZE:** (5) Sony Color TV's. **SECOND PRIZE:** (10) Litton Microwave Ovens. **THIRD PRIZE:** (20) Polaroid SX-70 Cameras. **FOURTH PRIZE:** (1000) Novus Calculators. **OPEN TO:** U.S. residents, including residents of Florida. **VOID:** Missouri, Ohio, Utah, Vermont, and wherever prohibited by law. **DEADLINE:** Entries must be postmarked by October 17, 1977. **HOW TO ENTER:** On an Official Entry Form or 3" x 5" plain piece of paper, handprint your name, address, zip code, and phone number. Each entry submitted must be accompanied by either of the following: two (2) wrappers from any size of Safeguard, or a 3" or 5" plain piece of paper on which you have printed the words "Safeguard's Smallest Soapstakes." Enter as often as you wish, but mail each entry separately in a hand-addressed envelope no larger than a 1/8" x 9 1/2" (#10 envelope) to: Safeguard's Smallest Soapstakes, P.O. Box 1831, Blair, Nebraska 68009. Sweepstake participation via entry blanks distributed in retail stores is void in Wisconsin, Maryland, West Virginia, and South Dakota.

Contest promotions usually advertise three to five months before their deadline dates. Why get in a dither and frustrated when you can address and prepare your entries using the following method:

(a) After reading the Rules, decide how many you want to send.

(b) Get your envelopes from your stored supply and address one envelope this way:

Wherever I intend to paste the stamp, I write the date I want to start mailing, and when I want to mail my last entry.

(c) Next, count out 3" x 5" pieces of paper and with a rubberband secure them with the fifty envelopes. Fifty pieces of paper are for printing your name, address, zip code, and telephone number. The other fifty are for printing the words: "Safeguard's Smallest Soapstakes." When you have free time you can address your envelopes. Be sure to handprint the envelopes as the rules indicated.

When I watch TV, sit under the dryer at the beauty parlor, or in the car on the way to our lake cabin with my husband, I usually have two or three packets ready to be addressed. It's really an easy, simple way to enter contests, when you follow a system. When I am finished with my addressing, it only takes a few minutes to file them. I use this procedure in all the contests I enter.

If I find entry blanks in grocery stores or drug stores, I use them. Magazines many times carry contest rules. I have found from experience, that whether you use an official entry blank or a 3" x 5" piece of paper or card, makes absolutely no difference in your chances of winning. The main thing is to enter. Whether you send in two, twenty, or two hundred, try to enter every contest that comes along; that is, if you're interested in the prizes offered.

When To Mail Entries

Some people like to mail their entries all at once at the beginning, middle, or end of the contest. Judging firms claim that over half of the entries submitted in contests come in the last, two weeks before deadline.

This is the method I use for mailing entries: after I address the envelopes, I space them in my file box at several different times before the last mailing date. In the Safeguard contest, the closing date was October 17. I had my fifty envelopes addressed on September 18. I spaced them between September 18 and the postmarked date of October 17. Some days I mailed two, some days one, and some days more. I use this method, because I like to have a chance of getting in more than one mail bag. Let me explain what I mean by, "...getting my entries into one or more mail bags."

In my research and reading on how sweep-stakes are selected, I became aware of the following information: On the day a sweepstake's drawing is held by the judging agency, the canvas mail sacks, full of entries, are numbered. If there are fifty sacks, then fifty slips of paper are placed in a metal, selection drum, numbered 1 to 50. Each numbered slip of paper represents a corresponding numbered mail sack.

To select the grand-prize winner, an executive from the judging firm is blindfolded and led to the selection drum. The drum is rotated several times, to insure random selection. The executive reaches through the hinged opening at the top of the drum, and retrieves a single piece of paper. The number is read and, still blindfolded, the person doing the drawing is led to the mail sack with the corresponding number. They reach in and pull out one envelope. The selection of entries is continued in this manner until all winners of the contest are drawn.

Postmark is checked to insure compliance with the closing date. Five out of every hundred entries selected as winners are disqualified (why?), the reasons being: using incorrect size of 3" x 5" paper; using a rubber stamp to indicate name and address, when the rules require the entrant to "print" that information; writing in script-style instead of printing; entries postmarked after closing date; failure to indicate on the entry form the name and address of the store where entry blank was obtained or where you shop. This question is often asked and the answer just had to be included.

The majority of winners use a 3" x 5" piece of paper instead of an official entry blank. Only a small number of winning entries contain box top or wrapper. Most winners use a substitute of a 3" x 5" to print the product name.

When You Get An Affidavit

When you win a contest and receive written notification from the judging firm or sponsor, sometimes you are required to sign a form to verify your name, address, and social security number. You are asked to have it notarized, and returned in the self-addressed envelope that is enclosed. If a copy for your files is not included, make a photostat. If you don't receive a prize or hear from the company in a reasonable length of time, you will know where to write.

When To Project And Give Energy

When you do the writing and addressing of the envelopes for a certain contest, paint a mental picture of the prize you want to win. When you mail the envelope, give it energy that it will be the winner. When it comes to your mind, and it will, again see yourself as already having and enjoying the prize.

LOOK FOR EXCITING THINGS TO HAPPEN, BECAUSE THEY WILL.

Contesting: The Name It and Claim It Game

Chapter Sixteen

The Questions Most Often Asked By Students

The Questions Most Often Asked By Students

1. What about income tax?

Contest winnings, with expenses deducted, are treated as ordinary income. Don't begrudge paying your taxes. Seventy-five per cent of something is better than one hundred per cent of nothing. Consult your IRS for specific cases.

2. When will they let me know I won?

After the winners are selected by the judging

firm, the sponsor prints a list of the winners and will mail you a copy, if you request it and send a self-addressed stamped envelope.

It may be a week or two after the contest is judged before you are notified. You may get a phone call (if it is a large prize), or you may get a letter telling you of your win. If it is one of the smaller prizes you won, you simply get the package of whatever it is, and a note saying this is your prize for entering their contest. I have received packages three months after the close of a contest. So there is no set pattern or time for you to hear. Send for the winner's list if you want to make certain you did or did not win in a particular contest.

3. Is it necessary to use a return address on my mailing envelope?

No, this is not necessary. If you do not use one, you may print, write, use a rubber stamp, or sticker. If you're sending in lots of entries, you'll find it time-consuming to use it. Do be sure the address you're sending to is correct.

4. May I abbreviate the mailing **address** to **save** time?

Yes. Be careful what you abbreviate, though. You may abbreviate the "Post Office Box" to simply

"Box," and you may also abbreviate the state name. If you are sending thirty entries to Massachusetts, you'll save lots of time by simply using **MA.**

5. Does it help to use colored envelopes when entering sweepstakes?

No. The drawings are made by someone who is blindfolded. Therefore, any special colors, decorations, etc. are of no real advantage. Colored envelopes are also more expensive than plain white ones. I will say that if you BELIEVE colored envelopes will help you win, then you are directing more energy towards your win. Then it is your BELIEF (positive thinking) that is helping make it happen, rather than the color.

6. What is the difference between handprinting, writing and block letters?

"Write" means to write in cursive, as you would sign your name. "Handprint" means you must print the required information by hand, not using a typewriter, stamp, or computer. If the rules say you must "print" or "handprint" in block letters, this means you must use ALL CAPITAL LETTERS. They don't have to be a work of art—just legible.

7.   What is considered to be a plain piece of paper? Does the color matter? Is a card acceptable?

The color of the paper you use makes no difference unless the rules call for a certain color (which is rare).

A "plain piece of paper" is simply that—a plain piece of paper. No lines. No decorations. Again, color makes no difference unless specified. If the rules request a "piece of paper," then it may have lines, etc.

Usually, the rules will specify your paper to be a certain size (3" x 5" is the most common). In this case, be sure your paper is "3 x 5," not "3 1/4 x 5." Judging firms are sticklers on rules. Some even measure to see if the paper or card is 3" or 5". I understand they'll allow 1/8" difference.

Some judges will accept a card in place of a piece of paper. But be safe rather than sorry. When the rules request paper, use paper. If they request a card, then use a card. You can always feel safe when you follow the rules EXACTLY!

8. What is the best-sized envelope to use?

The #10 (4 1/8" x 9 1/2") is probably best. It gives you the largest size without running the risk of being rejected. Some people will use very large manila envelopes. Naturally this gives these entries an advantage. I'm sure this is the reason more and more rules are specifying an envelope "no larger than 4 1/8" x 9 1/2" (#10 envelope). You may, of course, use smaller envelopes. There isn't much price difference per envelope between a #10 and a #6 3/4.

9. Is it necessary to print the quote marks around the words to be printed?

Let's use an example. The rules say to print the words "Safeguard's Smallest Soapstakes" on a 3"x 5" piece of paper. Here the quote marks are used to set aside the words to be printed from the rest of the words in the sentence. You may or may not want to use quote marks in this instance. In another case, the rules may say to print the words: Dove's "Beautiful You" Sweepstakes. In this case, I would definitely use them, since they are within a phrase to be printed.

10. Are the "Second Chance Sweepstakes" worth entering—or are most prizes awarded to "Instant Winners"?

Few, if any, prizes are usually won in "Instant Winner" portions of sweepstakes. This means there are still many prizes still to be awarded in the "Second Chance Sweepstakes," which makes it worth entering.

11. Can I send entries in someone else's name?

Yes, but be sure they meet all the qualifications of the sweepstakes. The state in which they live must not be a "void" state. And they must meet all other personal requirements that may be in the rules, such as age, licensed driver, etc. Keep in mind that if their name is drawn as a winner, the prize is awarded in their name, it must be reported on their income tax, and they may also have to pay taxes on the prize. All these things should be considered before you proceed.

12. What does it mean when the rules say the prizes are non-transferable?

It simply means the prize is awarded in the name of and to the person whose name is drawn as a winner. It will not be awarded in another person's name, even if requested. After the prize has been awarded, the winner may do whatever he or she wishes: keep it, sell it, or give it away.

14. How do you decide how many entries you want to mail on a particular contest?

I look at the prize list. If something excites me, like a trip to Hawaii, I may send fifty entries.

Someone suggested this method of deciding how many entries to submit in each sweepstakes: Don't spend any more in postage than the value of the last prize. It's a rule of thumb, but not always applicable.

You may find it helpful to set up a sweepstake's budget, allowing so much per month for postage. For example: you allow $25 per month. This means you can send in one hundred entries per month—which is about three entries per day. The consistent winners enter often and consistently.

15. Which contests/sweepstakes should I send my entries to, since there are so many?

First, the prizes should be prizes you would like to win. So, set yourself some prize goals like my family and I always have, then concentrate your entries on the contests and sweepstakes offering these prizes.

16. Do entries with the "Official Entry Blank" and proof-of-purchase stand a better chance of winning than those using a 3" x 5" substitute?

NO! It's just like colored envelopes. Drawings are made blindfolded and at random. In fact, most winners use the substitutes since the official entry blanks can be hard to find in large quantities. The same goes for the proof-of-purchase and its' substitute. When entering sweepstakes, you are not required to make a purchase. When a sweepstake asks for a proof-of-purchase (box top, end flap, wrapper, etc.), you will always find a substitute qualifier (proof-of-purchase) allowed. This is usually a 3" x 5" card with certain information required to be printed or written.

17. Are my chances of winning better in local contests and sweepstakes?

Definitely. You don't have as much competition, since entries are restricted to fewer people, in comparison with the national ones. Your local radio, TV, and newspaper should be paid attention to for these promotions. Use the same principles in these as you do in the national ones.

18. How many contests can you recall winning?

All of them. Life is a contest and I consider myself a WINNER. Be it merchandise, a job, a health problem, or whatever. I certainly will not give up until I accomplish what I set out to do. To me there are no failures, only a delay in results. When I accomplish one of my projects, I go on to another.

19. "I just finished reading a book on a positive-principle outlook. It stated, 'Pray for what you will, but be willing to take what God gives you.' What do you think of that suggestion? As a child I was told it's the will of God for some people to be poor, and supposedly we were one of those 'unfortunate' families. I did not believe what I was being told, so I was on a search to find out what the real 'truth' was." (This is a direct quote from a letter I received.)

The book you read and quoted from was the opinion of the author. My book is my opinion from my experiences to date. You too, have an opinion and free will, and inwardly you know what is good for you. If your parents accepted poverty because they felt it was God's will, then that was their opinion and the limitation they placed on themselves. Whenever we reach the point of no return and say to ourselves, 'There has to be something more," we begin to make progress. Each day is a new day, a new beginning. We should never dwell in the past, except to realize what a fantastic learning experience we grew from.

I too, was raised amid poverty, limitation, and religious dogma that kept me in bondage with guilt.

I could not accept it, so I ventured out of the environment to do my own thing. I no longer accept or reject people or their opinions. I understand them. A number of years ago I was given a copy of someone's concepts titled, "Desiderata." I found so much encouragement, truth, and good sense in the writing, I keep a copy above my desk in my office, lest I forget what this life is all about.

20. Would you answer if I wrote you a letter to ask you something?

It depends on the letter. Many times it is not necessary. Someone may just write to tell me they won a trip after reading the book, and they are getting a new outlook on life. Some have health problems and ask for energy to help them face or heal a situation.

If you have a number of questions and it warrants a reply, just send a self-addressed, stamped envelope, for I usually answer by return mail. This I don't mind doing because we are here to help each other.

21. Does ESP have anything to do with contest winning? How does one develop it?

Extra Sensory Perception or *Effective Sensory Projection,* yes, does help. The majority of people still think ESP means Extra Sensory Perception, that few people have it, and you have ESP only if you can tell how many pennies someone has in his pocket.

Effective Sensory Projection is nothing but projecting energy toward an end result, seeing it as already having it. Now anyone can do that. *Effective Sensory Perception* is just being aware of people and things around you. You can read people simply by listening to them, watching their body mannerisms.

If you are interested or have the desire to cultivate your ESP power, then do it. The more observant you become, the more you will come to realize that there is really nothing hidden. It's just that you never noticed it before.

22. To what do you attribute your luck, or is it luck?

Yes, there is LUCK, but you make your own luck with a positive attitude. One of the contest judges that met a number of top winners had this to say, 'The big winners that I met and talked to all seem to have a positive attitude in all areas of their life." So if you want to be lucky, and have not been in the past, change your thinking and luck will follow.

23. Is the pursuit of material things selfish?

To some people, yes, if they think it is? For me, no. My concept of a selfish person is one that continues to want and accumulate things for the sheer joy of hoarding. When a person does not share, nor does he wish for anyone else to win or benefit from information, that person is selfish. To have creature comforts, good health, and happiness is everyone's birthright. Claim it.

24. Can winning lead to happiness when you know so many lose?

Everyone has the same opportunity to find their place in the FUN, if it's important enough to them. They can wallow in self-pity, be a BORN LOSER, but who keeps them there? They do. Of course being a winner is fun. It's not a "thing" that brings happiness, it's the person's attitude that determines that. Who was it that once said, "I would rather be rich and unhappy than poor and unhappy"? Think about it.

25. Why do different sweepstakes have different Post Office Boxes?

This is a way the sponsors key their sweepstakes advertising to measure responses from different parts of the country. It is a good idea to send your entries to different Post Offices when you have this information. It will help get your entries into different mail sacks for the drawing.

26. Can I win more than one prize in a contest or sweepstake?

Usually not. The rules will usually specify "...only one prize per person (or household)." This means no matter how many entries you sent or how many times your name was drawn, you can only win one prize.

27. Can i send more than one entry in an envelope in order to cut down on my postage?

Never—unless stated otherwise—and I've never seen it. Entries should always be mailed in separate envelopes, unless the rules state otherwise.

28. When using a 3" x 5" paper or card for my name and address (instead of the official entry blank), can I print the other required information on the same 3" x 5" card?

Unless the rules state to print all required information on one 3" x 5" piece of paper, use two pieces. One as a substitute for the official entry blank and the other for your qualifier or proof-of-purchase substitute.

29. When the rules state you must use an official entry blank, and I can't find any, how can I obtain them?

The best thing to do is write to the sponsoring company with attention to the Advertising Department. Explain that you would like to enter their contest or sweepstake, but cannot find the blanks locally. Ask for them to send a few and be sure to enclose a self-addressed, stamped envelope. Allow several weeks for their reply.

30. I noticed on some entry blanks there is a space for my phone number, but the official rules make no mention of having to print this if using a 3" x 5" substitute. Should I include it anyway?

If the official rules do not specify the need for your phone number, then it is not necessary—even though the official entry blank has space for one. Feel safe by following those printed official rules.

31. How can I find out about all the contests and sweepstakes around the country?

Subscribe to a contest bulletin. I subscribe to several.

32. Do I have to send for a winner's list in order to find out if I've won and to claim my prize?

No. The company will contact you if you have won a prize. You may wish to send for a winner's list for those contests and sweepstakes which you enter, just to be sure.

33. What is the "Universal Product Code" number requested in some sweepstakes?

It is the number appearing under the vertical bars on product packages.

34. How do I know contests and sweepstakes are legal?

They are closely monitored by the Federal Trade Commission. When drawings are held, a representative from the FTC or the US Postal Commission is present for observation. You can be assured the prizes will be awarded since a company would not spend a small fortune on sweepstake's advertising, then lose their reputation by not following through.

Contesting: The Name It and Claim It Game

Chapter
Seventeen

How To Be
A Winner
In All Areas
Of Your
Life

Contesting: The Name It and Claim It Game

HOW TO BE
A WINNER IN
ALL AREAS
OF YOUR LIFE

Some of you reading this book may have read material of a similar nature. Perhaps, you have been interested in entering contests and sweepstakes as a hobby, but somehow there were other projects that came first. You may be toying with the idea of getting serious and making the time for contesting on a regular basis. Don't be discouraged...sometimes new ideas have to be presented a number of times before we accept them.

I must share an interesting observation from one of my friends, Dr. Joseph Murphy, who has written over fortythree books on the power of mind. While lecturing in the Dallas area, he came to my home on several occasions. Because he was a down-to-earth sort of person, I felt free to voice my opinions on his books and subject matter.

One day I commented. "Murphy, I find your books easy to read and understand, but I notice you say the same thing over and over again. In some of your books, you even repeat the same examples verbatim."

With a grin and twinkle in his steel blue eyes, he replied, "Well, Helen, I figure if some people read something fortythree times they may finally get it." Repetition, many times, is the only way learning can be accomplished for some.

Recently I received a letter from a young mother in Kansas. She started out by telling how she enjoyed reading *THE NAME IT AND CLAIM IT GAME*. She entered a few contests and intended making it a rewarding hobby. That was three years ago. Personal family problems became so challenging, she let it go by the wayside. Several months ago, after a divorce and a move, as she was sorting out her belongings, she rediscovered my book as she was unpacking boxes. She stopped to reread some pages, and became aware of something she had not noticed before.

"It was like reading a different book," she explained. "I realized what an upbeat sense of humor and attitude you have in all areas. NO FAILURE, ONLY A DELAY IN RESULTS stood out and I now have borrowed that phrase for my temporary holdups. Sure I want to win cars, trips, and money, and I will, but I KNOW what you were talking about when you said that we are all winners, but some of us have not realized it yet."

She continued. "It's only been a couple of months since I've read the book for the second time. I now continue to review it and find new ideas. I borrowed some of your 'gems of wisdom' as you call them, and I find myself repeating them daily. THOUGHTS BECOME THINGS...CONCEIVE IT..BELIEVE IT..ACHIEVE IT. This is one I really like, 'LIFE IS EITHER A DARING ADVENTURE OR NOTHING,' and 'PREPARE FOR YOUR GOOD.' and 'WHAT GOD HAS DONE FOR OTHERS, HE NOW DOES FOR ME AND MORE.'"

"The phrases I mentioned above are tacked around our apartment for me and my two sons, ages nine and eleven, to read. I know my attitude has changed, and my sons are cultivating more confidence and a better attitude, also."

"Last Saturday my nine-year-old son's name was drawn at the grocery store where we shop. He won a $50 merchandise certificate. He is having great fun planning how he will spend it. Monday, my eleven year old heard his name on the radio after sending in a post card. He won dinner for two and a collection of records. Now it's my turn."

"My writing to you today has a two-fold purpose. First to thank you for the super book you have written, and also to ask if you have more ideas about ways one can stay positive, constructive, and creative. I feel I've not been the best model in the past with my "martyr" attitude. You notice I said in the PAST. I assure you, that is where it will remain," she concluded.

It's letters like this that make my day.

Over my years of counseling people with all sorts of projects, I have compiled some ideas and techniques one can apply to suit one's particular needs. I feel we all have the power to create our own destinies, and that we can help ourselves along the way by constructive thinking and actions. Why not tune into our creative forces and make this a more positive environment, for ourselves and for those around us?

The more you are aware of your thoughts and

the more positive you are, the stronger and more powerful you become. Also, you will find your positive end results happening faster. The two most important things before beginning any venture is to KNOW what you want...and to STAY with it until it is realized. When the thought comes to your mind, picture yourself as already having it.

HOW TO DEVELOP PICTURE POWER

If you have difficulty picturing a goal by imagining it, then cut out pictures to depict what it is you want. Paste the pictures on a piece of cardboard. Tack the pictures up on the wall or door, wherever you will see them often. Every time you look at the pictures, pretend you already have what you want. You are giving your goals energy this way. Continue your imaging until your goal is realized.

SNAPPING FROM NEGATIVE TO POSITIVE THINKING

Wear a rubberband around your wrist and snap it every time you think or say something negative. Your negativity might manifest as follows: You may be irritable, dislike being around somebody, or get impatient. You may dwell on a physical problem and exaggerate it. You may feel depressed, entertain unfounded fears, feel lonely, unworthy, or "poor me" nobody likes or understands me. Every time your thinking becomes negative, snap the rubberband and change to positive thinking. You know what most of your DOWNERS are. Why not make a list of some of the positives?

I TRUST MY GOOD JUDGMENT WHEN MAKING DECISIONS.

I HAVE PERFECT VISION AND CAN SEE THINGS CLEARLY.

I AM BALANCED PHYSICALLY, MENTALLY, AND SPIRITUALLY.

I SHARE MY CONCEPTS IN A LOVING, HELPFUL WAY.

I RESPECT OTHERS' OPINIONS.

MY EMOTIONS ARE ALWAYS UNDER CONTROL

I RELEASE ANY OLD, LIMITING HABITS AND REPLACE THEM WITH NEW, UPLIFTING ONES

These are some ideas you may want to concentrate on to get started. Negative thinking can sap your energy and creativity, and prevent you from realizing your goals.

You will find it is fun being creative, and very quickly it can become a way of life for you. Become a positive, happy person. You will have more friends and be more content.

Contesting: The Name It and Claim It Game

UPLIFTING SAYINGS

Clip out every uplifting, humorous, or familiar phrase you read in papers or magazines. Type them on a piece of paper and cut the paper to measure one inch wide by three inches long. Cut a plastic straw into 1/2 inch pieces. Roll the typed-out, uplifting , humorous sayings around a toothpick and insert into the 1/2 inch straw. Place the sayings in a box or bowl and select several a day to read or meditate on. After reading, place them back into the container and keep adding to your collection. Soon you will be able to memorize them. I make boxes of uplifting sayings as personal gifts for my friends. Paste this message on the inside cover:

If its an answer you wish to find Let
it come from your subconscious mind
your hand will select the, answer or
clue To accept or reject is up to you!

Guests and friends enjoy selecting and reading the uplifting or humorous messages. I place my rolled messages in a crystal compote bowl, twelve inches high. It sits on my coffee table. To give you an idea what messages I clip:

222

"Humor is a hole that lets the sawdust out of a stuffed shirt."
—Jan McKeithen

It's hard to soar with eagles when you work with turkeys.

Are you aware that when you reach the bottom the next step is always UP?

Please be Patient... God isn't with you yet!

TO MEDITATE, do nothing more.

The PAST is dead, the FUTURE is God's, The PRESENT is ours!

"Who lives content with little, possesses everything."
—Despreaux

A man doesn't live by bread alone: he needs buttering up once in a while.

Its easier to suffer in silence if you are sure someone is watching

Ask and You Shall Receive

"All that some people leave on the sands of time are seatprints."
—David Vincent

"Plastic surgery can do anything with the human nose except keep it out of other people's business."
—S. A. Norris

"All mankind is divided into three classes: those who are immovable; those who are movable; and those who move." —Benjamin Franklin

The BIGGEST step you can take is the one you take when you meet the other person halfway.

"The best way to get a friend, is to be one."
— Frank Clark

"The more a man knows, the more he forgives."
—Catherine the Great

When all else fails, lower your standards!

"PEACE is happiness digesting."
—Victor Hugo

Some people are like boats: they toot the loudest when they're in a fog.

BE DIFFERENT.
ACT NORMAL!

224

Luck is like a rubber crutch: It will let you down when you try to lean on it.

"FRIENDSHIP is like a treasury: you cannot take from it more than you put into it." —Mandelstamm

"Anybody who isn't pulling his weight is probably pushing luck." :—Franklin P. Jones

Today...I will listen, learn and UNDERSTAND all things I come in contact with.

OPEN your heart and share all things with the LORD, and you will never walk alone.

It is better to wear out than rust out.

"Life is beautiful when one sees beyond it." —Bonnat

The very first step toward success in any job is to become interested in it.

When we do more, and ask for less—our lives are often more, fully blessed!

"It's hard to detect good luck— it looks so much like something you earned." —Frank Clark

225

THE BEGINNING OF WISDOM IS SILENCE.

Even the EGOTIST is to be admired —he never goes around talking about others.

The truth may set you free, but it won't make you many friends.

"Never try to make anyone like you ,you know and God knows, that one of you is enough"
—Emerson

"Where love rules there is no will to power."
—Carl Jung

Argue for your limitations, and sure enough, they're yours.
—Richard Bach

We will find time for anything we care enough about.

A GIFT must be given with LOVE , or it is no gift at all.

How a man plays the game shows something of his character; how he loses shows all of it.

Open your mind
—the mind
is the doorway
to the SOUL.

226

Contesting: The Name It and Claim It Game

Chapter Nineteen

How To Reinforce Your Talents and Greatness

Contesting: The Name It and Claim It Game

How To Reinforce Your Talents and Greatness

Make a fifteen-minute tape. Include every constructive, positive suggestion you can think about. There are many excellent suggestions in self-help books. Listen to the tape before you go to sleep at night. Before getting out of bed in the morning, tell yourself: 'Today is the first day of the rest of my life,
[1] and it will be the greatest experience yet." It will be.

I read a most interesting article in one of the tape catalogues I received in the mail. It stated that the average person remembers only 75 percent of any information they hear after a 24-hour period. After 48 hours, they only remember 50 percent. After 4 days they can recall only 15 percent, and after 16 days, they will remember only 2 percent of the original information. The article pointed out that in order to recall 62 percent of any information after several months, a person must hear something repeated 6 times or more. For this reason, I suggest listening to the tape nightly, for at least a month. This will almost guarantee you that not only will your thinking change, but your attitude will also. Remember— *YOU ARE WHAT YOU THINK.*

I'm aware I shared Frank Outlaw's profound statement in an earlier part of this book, but it's worth repeating at this time. *"Watch your thoughts, they become words; watch your words, they become actions; watch your actions, they become habits: watch your habits, they become character; watch your character, for it becomes your destiny."*

HOW TO GET OUT OF A RUT OR OUT OF DEPRESSION

Relax in a comfortable position. Breath deeply, and mentally repeat: "With each breath, I am cleansing myself of worry, pain, envy, hate (or whatever you want to eliminate.)" This should only take about five minutes of your time. There are so many little things one can do to keep happy, keep an uplifting outlook on life. By all means walk the malls, the park; visit a friend; or exercise. Share only happy situations with friends, avoid dwelling on your problems—they are only "projects" that you can solve. A wise man once said: *"Don't tell people your problems. Fifty percent could care less, and the other fifty percent are glad you got 'em."* Give that some thought.

DRAWING MONEY TO YOU

Buy a package of play money from the toy or game department of a store. Write your name on all the bills. Paste them on a piece of green cardboard. With a marks-a-lot, print: MY GOOD IS **AT HAND AND I AM** GRATEFULLY RECEIVING IT NOW. MONEY IS DRAWN TO ME CONSTANTLY. MY MONEY SUPPLY IS LIMITLESS. Read it several times each day and imagine you have a handfull of money. There is also an excellent audiocassette by Dr. Tag Powell, titled *THINK MONEY*. It can be obtained at any major bookstore, (the store where you purchased this book), or by mail from Top Of The Mountain Publishing.

HOW ABOUT LOTTERIES?

That's a question I am asked quite frequently. I don't know. I never have had an opportunity to do research. Texas does not have a state lottery. I do have some thoughts about how I would approach that sweepstake, if Texas should get a lottery. I would choose the numbers that had personal significance for me: my birthdate, house number, or social security number. I would stay with the same numbers, and keep giving energy to them by seeing myself being presented with a hefty amount on a check. It would be difficult to specify a certain amount, because I understand the jackpot varies. Each state has different systems and some use six numbers, some use eight. If your state lottery numbers are selected by TV, you certainly have an excellent opportunity to play the mind over matter game, and mentally see your numbers being selected. The more positive one becomes, the faster the end results are realized.

Chapter Eighteen

Contesting: The Name It and Claim It Game

Chapter Nineteen

How To Improve Your Child's Confidence By Using Their Creativity To Win Contest

Contesting: The Name It and Claim It Game

Contesting
For
Kids

As for contesting or entering sweepstakes...I now get great pleasure encouraging my grandson in these areas. He is showing an interest in the hobby.

When my grandson was eight years old, he spent some of his Summer vacation with me. I kept him busy being creative. The coloring contests he submitted paid off for him. In all, he entered five contests. He won three: $100 for a national magazine for drawing and coloring a picture of his family;

a second prize in another for coloring a pirate (the prize was a videocassette recorder with twelve videos); and a cereal box contest awarded him $100.

COLORING CONTESTS

In a coloring contest, you simply use crayons and color the picture. You read the rules carefully. Rules usually list how the picture will be judged, example: creative use of coloring materials 30 percent; overall artistic effect 30 percent; interpretation of elements in the picture 20 percent; neatness 20 percent.

Let's explain. With all the crayon colors available and different shades of the same color, you have an opportunity to make pictures more creative with light and dark blends. Be more creative and embellish with interesting effects. A picture may have a beach scene: Why not color the sand tan, put a thin coat of glue over it, and sprinkle that part of the picture with real sand! To present a "3-D" effect entry: cut out the main character and paste it on a piece of cardboard; paste the back scene in a box the size of the picture. (Boxes can be purchased at any variety store in the "gift wrap" department.) You may want to glue in plastic greenery of small sizes, to give it depth. Visit the craft department of any variety store for many, more ideas. You may want to use round eyes that move. If people are in the picture that you are to color, you might want to dress them with dress material or blue jean material. How about

241

using yarn for the hair? Some materials have a shaggy texture, that could be used on animals. If a water scene is in the picture, color it shades of blue. It gives the water a real wet look. Yes, there is a place for glitter, too. But children tend to go overboard. For Christmas and Winter scenes it is okay, in moderation.

How about a night scene, to be different? If so, use deep blue for the sky and spangles for stars. Bear in mind that children's coloring contests are very popular and the judges receive thousands of entries. After awhile, they all start to look alike to the judges, so *yours must be different.*

For young children in the five to seven age bracket, let them look in coloring books to get ideas. If it calls for a drawing, they can get some ideas from them. Using an example is better than giving them a blank sheet of paper.

What did my grandson submit to win the $100 for the contest that required children to draw a picture of their family? After encouraging him to page through story and coloring books, he decided on the illustration below. This is a copy of what he submitted. I made a copy from the original and added it to his GROWING UP scrapbook.

He used graph paper and a ruler to keep the picture neat. He pictured himself in his little league shirt and cap. When it came to drawing Mom, "She is always on the phone," he commented. It took several days to complete the drawing and coloring, with plenty of encouragement. When it was finished and mailed, I had to remind him that it would take several months before he might hear from the judges. I also reminded him to see himself opening the envelope and getting a check. Prizes in this contest were money. It took almost three months after closing date before he received his $100 prize.

Judging firms will send out a winner's list if you request it. Some people like to know who won. If this interests you, you must send a self-addressed, stamped envelope and be sure to read the rules—the address to receive a winner's list is different from the address where you submit the coloring entry.

The other contest my grandson entered required him to color a picture of a pirate. The pirate was sitting on a beach. He did use real sand for the beach and after coloring the water blue, he put an overcoat of clear nail polish. He enjoys writing stories

so he wanted to make his entry like a storybook. He used a folder and printed the title of the story on the cover: "PETE THE KINDHEARTED PIRATE." He really was excited with this project, because the big prize was a family trip and a chest full of toys.

He received an affidavit the first of December. In January, he received a letter telling him he won second prize, a videocassette recorder with twelve videos. In February, the prize was delivered.

Many times, a package will arrive with just a note saying you won the prize. So it can be very exciting for children if they make coloring and drawing contests their hobby.

This year, our grandson was declared the most artistic student in his class of thirty. His painting of birds was displayed at the Civic Art Center. For that, he received a gold ribbon and his picture in the paper. Prior to entering coloring contests, he was not that interested in being creative. Encourage children while they are young. It not only can be profitable, but it develops talent in the artistic areas.

Contesting: The Name It and Claim It Game

"LIFE IS EITHER A DARING ADVENTURE OR NOTHING"

The publication of this book was an adventure for me. I had to crawl way out on the end of a long limb, and self-publish the first edition, not knowing what the results might be. Looking back at that decision, I can see how much it changed my whole life. (Almost a million copies of the original book, plus revisions, have been sold.) I've met fascinating people, traveled all over the world, and now enjoy teaching at my own center in Alvardo, Texas.

Contesting: The Name It and Claim It Game

Some of the exciting highlights that come to mind are: In 1973 i was invited to Prague to presort a paper on some ideas J have on aberrations and thought forms. I had DEJA VU while in a palace in Moscow. Also, while in the Roman catacombs I had a hairy and scary "reviewing" my tomb.

On November 12, 1986 I left for Peru to do some lecturing and workshops. I planned on a ten-day stay. I was there until January 20 of 1987. It would take a book to share my experiences during my stay there. Later, in July, I spent three weeks in Sedona, Arizona, to find out for myself, the rumors about the energy vortexes. I am going to reserve my opinion on that experience for a future date. Perhaps I have a vivid imagination, but life is real for me. Someone remarked recently, that SHIRLEY MACLAINE BETTER MOVE OVER...because Helen Hadsell is a COSMIC ROVER, too.

I feel so fortunate to be on planet Earth at this time, with the stepping up of awareness, and the untapped power of the mind that is waiting to be re-discovered. All my days and experiences are re-warding, uplifting, and exciting.

May yours also be.

Contesting: The Name It and Claim It Game

ABOUT THE AUTHOR

If you give your wishes enough energy, they will manifest.
This is not just wishful thinking; it's a fact

Helen Hadsell is living proof not only of her own dynamic philosophy of life, but of the entire New Thought Movement emphasis on successful living through right thinking. Her practice of positive thinking in the energetic pursuit of her goals has brought her rich rewards in terms of spiritual, physical, and material well-being. This book, *Contesting: The Name It And Claim It Game,* is her own, true account of the amazing events in her life that bear out her conviction that anyone can achieve anything their mind can conceive, if they firmly resolve to do so.

Mrs. Hadsell holds the unique record of having submitted a winning entry for every contest prize she has ever wanted—and they have been many. Her prizes, since the beginning of her contesting career in 1957, have included sports equipment,

253

electric appliances, a Hammond organ, and trips to New York, Washington, DC, and Europe; and of course, her dream home in a contest sponsored by the Formica Corporation.

By way of explanation for her uncanny, good fortune, she states: "I don't believe in luck and I don't believe in accidents. I project my goal on my mental screen. Then I give it nothing but positive energy."

The author has studied hypnotism and "Silva Mind Development," and has attended a number of seminars on parapsychology and hypnosis in Europe. She has appeared on national television and radio interview shows, and is currently writing and lecturing on positive thinking and ESP research. She believes that one of the great breakthroughs of the future will be that every individual can develop his "Psi-Q": controlled mental energy.

Mrs. Hadsell, mother of three, grown children, lives in Alvardo, Texas, with her husband, who shares her interest in helping people improve their lives through proper use of mental power.

Contesting: The Name It and Claim It Game

CONTESTING:
THE NAME IT AND CLAIM IT GAME

How to be a winner—in the contest at your supermarket or in the game of life.

Helen Hadsell, who is called "The woman who wins every contest prize she desires," shares her secrets in a manner: vibrant, warm, and folksy, that is unique to only her.

Sample the good life with Helen. She will cover the secrets for confidence and success, and how to visualize your success. Her use of metaphors from her experiences will help you clearly understand the principles of winning. Get the winning edge!

Learn the nuts and bolts information of contesting mechanics from how to save money on envelopes; how to create a winning entry—to how to win at the exciting game of life; with sections on building a confident, creative attitude in children, by showing them how to use their creative mind to win contests. You will enjoy Helen's personal thoughts on picking that winning lottery number, and how to build the Hadsell Answer Chest—a unique decision-making tool you develop yourself.

Underground Bestseller. Over a million copies sold. Secret weapon of the contest winners. Professional winners' choice. Who says you can't win 'em all!

ABOUT THE AUTHOR Helen Hadsell is living proof not only ofher own dynamic philosophy of life, but of the entire New Thought Movement emphasis on successful living through right thinking. Her practice of positive thinking in the energetic pursuit of her goals has brought her rich rewards in terms of spiritual, physical and material well-being. This book. *Contesting: The Name It And Claim It Game,* is her own, true account of the amazing events in her life that bear out her conviction that anyone can achieve anything their mind can conceive, if they firmly resolve to do so. Mrs. Hadsell holds the unique record of having submitted a winning entry for every contest prize she has ever wantecd—and there have been many. Her prizes, since the beginning of her contesting career in 1957, have included sports equipment, electric appliances, a Hammond organ, and trips to New York, Washington, DC, and Europe; and of course, her dream home in a contest sponsored by the Formica Corporation.

ISBN 0-914295-66-7